September–December 2014

Rooting women's lives in the Bible

Christina Press
BRF
Tunbridge Wells/Abingdon

Copyright © 2014 Christina Press and BRF
The Bible Reading Fellowship, 15 The Chambers, Vineyard, Abingdon OX14 3FE

First published in Great Britain 2014

ISBN 978 0 85746 043 1

Distributed in Australia by:
Mediacom Education Inc., PO Box 610, Unley, SA 5061.
Tel: 1800 811 311; Fax: 08 8297 8719;
E-mail: admin@mediacom.org.au

Distributed in New Zealand by:
Scripture Union Wholesale, PO Box 760, Wellington
Tel: 04 385 0421; Fax: 04 384 3990;
E-mail: suwholesale@clear.net.nz

Acknowledgments

Scripture quotations taken from The Holy Bible, New International Version (Anglicised edition), copyright © 1979, 1984, 2011 by Biblica (formerly International Bible Society). Used by permission of Hodder & Stoughton Publishers, an Hachette UK company. All rights reserved. 'NIV' is a registered trademark of Biblica (formerly International Bible Society). UK trademark number 1448790.

Scripture quotations taken from The New Revised Standard Version of the Bible, Anglicised Edition, copyright © 1989, 1995 by the Division of Christian Education of the National Council of the Churches of Christ in the United States of America, are used by permission. All rights reserved.

Scripture quotations from THE MESSAGE. Copyright © by Eugene H. Peterson 1993, 1994, 1995. Used by permission of NavPress Publishing Group.

Scripture quotations from the Holy Bible, New Living Translation, copyright © 1996, 2004. Used by permission of Tyndale House Publishers, Inc., Wheaton, Illinois 60189. All rights reserved.

Scriptures quoted from the Good News Bible published by The Bible Societies/HarperCollins Publishers Ltd, UK © American Bible Society 1966, 1971, 1976, 1992, used with permission.

Extracts from the Authorised Version of the Bible (The King James Bible), the rights in which are vested in the Crown, are reproduced by permission of the Crown's Patentee, Cambridge University Press.

New King James Version of the Bible copyright © 1979, 1980, 1982 by Thomas Nelson, Inc. All rights reserved.

Printed by Gutenberg Press, Tarxien, Malta.

Contents

Contributors

Tracy Williamson is an author and speaker working for a music and teaching ministry headed up by blind gospel singer Marilyn Baker. Tracy, who is deaf, shares a home with Marilyn. They travel the country giving concerts and leading conferences drawing people into wholeness through intimacy with God.

Sandra Wheatley lives in Newcastle-upon-Tyne and, despite the ongoing progression and challenges of MS, continues to enjoy swimming, praying, baking cakes and meeting with friends.

Mary Reid, now retired from teaching, publishing and editing, is actively involved, with her husband Gavin, in their local church and community.

Rosemary Green has recently moved to Abingdon, the home of BRF. She has four adult offspring and 14 grandchildren.

Margaret Killingray is now almost fully retired. She writes occasionally for the London Institute for Contemporary Christianity and for Scripture Union. She is married to a retired history professor and has eight grandchildren.

Christine Platt's passion for writing started in Ivory Coast, West Africa, where she worked with The Navigators. She now lives in New Zealand and travels regularly to East Timor to support the church there. She is writing Bible resources in one of their languages (Tetun).

Jennifer Rees Larcombe runs Beauty from Ashes, an organisation that supports people adjusting to bereavement and trauma.

Ali Herbert is a freelance writer and musician and also works as Communications Manager for St Stephen's Church in Twickenham. She is married to Nick and they have two children.

Alie Stibbe has been a freelance writer and translator for almost 20 years. Her books for BRF include *Barefoot in the Kitchen* and *A Spacious Place*. She lives in Watford, works at several jobs and is an active member of Watford Community Church.

Christina Rees is a writer, broadcaster and consultant, and a member of the General Synod and Archbishops' Council of the Church of England. Christina speaks and preaches widely and works to promote the vision of a restored humanity in Christ.

Catherine Butcher writes...

This year, the *Day by Day with God* theme is 'hope', to tie in with HOPE14—and initiative in which churches have been working together, with words and actions, to spread the hope that Jesus gives. By exploring the hope we have as Christians, we become better able to share that hope with others. Over the coming four months, ask God to fill you with fresh hope that overflows into the lives of others. Ask him for courage to put your faith into words, as well as the insight to see where loving action is needed. As Peter reminds us, 'Always be prepared to give an answer to everyone who asks you to give the reason for the hope that you have. But do this with gentleness and respect' (1 Peter 3:15).

For me, this is the last time I'll be introducing the notes. After ten years as editor of *Day by Day with God*, I am handing on the role. Writing these notes together with so many fantastic contributors over the past decade has meant we have shared our lives in a small way. I feel connected to each writer and to the many readers who take time to write to us at the BRF office. It has been a privilege to be part of your daily journey with Jesus.

The new editor of *Day by Day with God* is Ali Herbert—one of the contributors to this issue. I first met Ali at a women's conference run by *Day by Day with God* and *Woman Alive*. She is married to Nick, they have two children, and Ali works part-time as communications manager for her church in Twickenham. As we spent time together talking through the editor's tasks, it was an emotional moment for me to pray for Ali and hand on the baton.

Ali has already commissioned the January 2015 notes: do pray for her, asking God to give her wisdom as she seeks his guidance to set the themes for the series. She has graciously asked me to continue as a contributor, so you will be hearing from me again next November when I'll be looking at Nehemiah.

My ongoing prayer for us all is that we would come closer to Jesus every day, strengthened by his love and equipped to spread the hope he gives us with the people we meet. Wouldn't it be amazing to be used by God in this coming year to bring lasting change to lives in our communities?

Making links

Tracy Williamson writes:

You have been chosen. 'You are a chosen people, a royal priesthood, a holy nation, God's special possession, that you may declare the praises of him who called you out of darkness into his wonderful light' (1 Peter 2:9).

I love this week's theme, 'Chosen and transformed'. Transformation, living a truly joyful and peace-filled life, flows out of the fact that we are chosen, the opposite to being rejected. God has chosen you. He has picked you out and called you to belong to him. He has found something he cherishes and loves in you. How does that make you feel? What does it actually mean to you to be chosen?

Choosing is a fundamental part of life. We have to make choices at almost every moment. We choose whether to get up in the morning or to go back to sleep. We choose what to eat, what to wear, and what activities we will focus on during the day. Maybe you don't have much room for making choices in your job or home life, but choosing our inward mental or emotional responses is as crucial as choosing any outward actions—for example, how we will react to hurtful comments or whether we will reach out to someone or withdraw.

When God says through Peter that we are a 'chosen people', he is declaring a life-changing truth that can heal our hearts and release us into our true destinies if we seek to really believe and live by his words.

So this week we will look at some Bible characters who were radically transformed by God's choosing of them. As we read, we can let God touch us just as he touched them, for he has no favourites and says that we too are chosen to become his beloved children and heirs.

I pray that as you read, pray and reflect, you will be healed of all wounds of rejection and empowered to step out into all he has chosen you to be.

Chosen to receive healing love

[The woman] came trembling and fell at his feet. In the presence of all the people, she told why she had touched him and how she had been instantly healed. Then he said to her, 'Daughter, your faith has healed you. Go in peace.'

Some situations seem hopeless—illness or escalating conflicts with loved ones or a lifestyle that desperately needs changing.

Jesus wants to give you fresh hope today. He is our living hope and always desires to turn around the impossible and pour joy into our lives. Nothing is too difficult for him.

This woman had been bleeding for twelve years and had spent all her money seeking healing. With her condition, she couldn't ask for prayer in a meeting. She was ceremonially unclean and people shunned her lest they become unclean too. How deep her emotional pain must have been, to feel so isolated, with no hope of anything changing.

When hope seems to have been stripped away, God prompts us to throw ourselves on him. The woman pushed through the crowd, believing that if she could just touch Jesus' cloak she would be healed. When we consciously place ourselves in the presence of God, true hope is reborn. The woman chose to listen to and to act according to his promptings and was immediately healed, but Jesus was also making a choice. He chose not just to answer her obvious outward need but also to minister into her deepest longing for love and affirmation: 'Daughter, your faith has healed you. Go in peace.'

Jesus always chooses not to leave us in our brokenness. It can be scary to make ourselves vulnerable in front of others, to admit that we have needs, but Jesus loves us too much to let us stay hidden. Listen for his call of love. Come out from your hiding place. He wants to affirm the steps you've already taken and call you 'Daughter'. The woman was transformed by his choice to love her into wholeness. Let him love you into wholeness too.

Thank you, dear Lord Jesus, that with your hope in my heart I can find new strength to reach out to you with my need. Thank you that you are willing to answer in ways that are beyond what I can ever ask or imagine.
TRACY WILLIAMSON

Chosen to receive divine revelation

The woman said, 'I know that Messiah' (called Christ) 'is coming.
When he comes, he will explain everything to us.' Then Jesus
declared, 'I, the one speaking to you—I am he.'

This story is enthralling. It conveys dynamically the wonder of God's
mercy in choosing us despite our failures. He chooses us not just to be
recipients of his grace but to draw us into intimacy and give us divine
revelation that will both heal and empower us.

Maybe, like this woman, you've made wrong choices in life and, as a
result, are suffering shame or isolation. I love the way that Jesus, despite
being weary, responds to God's promptings and chooses to reach out to
her. She is obviously trying to avoid people but Jesus is not put off and
opens up a conversation with her.

When we feel shamed and aware of others' judgement, we withdraw
and become afraid. It seems impossible to believe that God still loves
and wants to speak to us, but he always does. Right now he is with you
and wanting to bathe you with his transforming love and understanding. Like that woman, you can be empowered by his words to step out
of your inner strongholds of fear or shame. Jesus had received revelation from the Holy Spirit about her deepest needs but the first thing he
said to her was 'Will you give me a drink?' (v. 7). How incredible that
he spoke first into the area of her anointing to serve, which had long
since shut down. He then declared, 'I, the one speaking to you—I am
he.'

What amazing love he showed in choosing to reveal the truth of his
divinity to a sinful woman, but this is the kind of revelation he calls
us all to experience. Knowing that he knows us completely, and then
receiving revelation about who he really is, sets us free. The woman was
transformed and empowered, and this is what we too will experience as
we open up to him.

---

*Dear Lord Jesus, thank you for the wonder of your knowledge of me.
Forgive me for trying to run away, and help me, just as you did that
woman, to live as the person you made me to be.*

TRACY WILLIAMSON

Chosen to do his works

[Jesus] said to Simon, 'Put out into deep water, and let down the nets for a catch.' Simon answered, 'Master, we've worked hard all night and haven't caught anything. But because you say so, I will let down the nets.'

I love Simon Peter because he was an ordinary man with a simple lifestyle. He was comfortingly real in his muddled reactions, at one moment full of confidence, at the next full of confusion or fear.

God had chosen Peter and loved him, just as he chooses and loves us. Jesus called him 'Rock' and persevered with him, despite knowing that Peter would later disown him. From the start he gave Peter significance by asking him for the use of his boat, but then astonished him with the amazing catch of fish.

We feel secure in familiar roles but we can cling to them too tightly. God wants us to have a kingdom mentality, to do his works. He has chosen us for greater things. Jesus said to Peter, 'Don't be afraid; from now on you will fish for people' (v. 10). He gave Peter a new level of understanding and power by using the very life experiences and terminology that Peter understood. He always meets us where we are, then challenges us to step out.

When Jesus was arrested and Peter fell back into fear, all seemed lost. He crept away and wept bitterly, his heart broken by his own fickleness (Luke 22:62). Those of us who are heartbroken, believing we have let God down too badly for him to ever to love or use us again, can draw comfort from the way Jesus healed Peter, in John 21:15–17. Jesus took him aside and, through their conversation, stripped his sins of their condemning power. Three times Jesus said, 'Feed my sheep, take care of my lambs.' He still trusted Peter and loved him. He still loves you and trusts you too.

We are chosen to do Jesus' works. He will use all our life experiences and gifts; nothing need be wasted. He longs for us to trust him and step out as he calls us.

Thank you for choosing me, dear Lord, and thank you for your trust in me. Please help me to be all you've called me to be.

TRACY WILLIAMSON

Chosen to be a great leader

'So now, go. I am sending you to Pharaoh to bring my people the Israelites out of Egypt.' But Moses said to God, 'Who am I that I should go to Pharaoh and bring the Israelites out of Egypt?' And God said, 'I will be with you.'

God chose Moses, but Moses also had to choose whether to accept God's calling or remain guilty and unfulfilled. I love the way God made himself known to Moses in the midst of the ordinary. God always meets us where we are, invading the mundane with heaven's glory. If only we are willing to stop, look and pray as Moses did when he examined the burning bush, we will be touched by God's grace in amazingly transformative ways.

Moses was in a desert place, both literally and spiritually. He had messed up his calling 40 years before by trying to fulfil it in his own strength and had ended up committing murder. When God met him, he was burnt out by regret and shame and could only say 'Who am I…?'

If you feel that deep sense of emptiness and regret, or if you are in a desert of loneliness, like Moses, remember that God has chosen you too and can transform your life. One night when I was very depressed, I sensed God prompting me to look at the stars. All I could see was black sky reflecting my hopelessness, but suddenly I saw a twinkling star and then innumerable diamonds spread across the sky. God spoke to me then that I was like those stars, shining in a black and empty universe with the beauty of his love. I knew that I had to choose whether to believe God and walk in my calling to be that shining star or stay in my prison of despair. Moses was full of excuses but did eventually 'hear' and respond to God's call. As for me, I know that God has chosen me and his transforming work is still ongoing in my life. How about you?

'God has called you. He has chosen you. He really loves you. He's always close beside you, and as you lean on him, he will give you the resources of heaven.' (© Marilyn Baker Music, 1994)

TRACY WILLIAMSON

Chosen for this moment

'And who knows but that you have come to royal position for such a time as this?'

Do you ever think, 'What difference can I make?' Sometimes I feel so despairing about our world that even praying seems futile, let alone believing I can change anything.

This sense of futility is a clever lie from Satan, who strives to persuade us that we are ineffective and to keep us from understanding our God-given royal authority. Fear is his weapon, and fear was Esther's immediate response when Mordecai first asked her to go to the king to plead for the Jews. She replied, 'For any man or woman who approaches the king… the king has but one law: that they be put to death' (4:11).

The fear that this law put into her was Esther's only focus. She was distressed for her people and her beloved uncle Mordecai, but she was bound by her sense of inadequacy. How often do we react to difficult situations like that? Tough circumstances in my early life robbed me of self-esteem and I often feel fear welling up in my heart with paralysing effect. Everything that could go wrong seems so much more of a certainty than a divine miracle.

When Mordecai challenged Esther, however, asking, 'Who knows but that you have come to royal position for such a time as this?' something shifted. She heard Mordecai's words as coming from God and suddenly knew that she was indeed chosen. She rose up, empowered by a calm wisdom to know how to undertake her momentous task.

We too are chosen by God. We are his royal representatives 'for such a time as this'. We must look to him rather than at the 'certainties' that make us fearful. We can have an incredible impact on our communities, our families, even the world, as we choose to pray and act out of the Holy Spirit's divine authority, which is our inheritance in Christ.

Father, thank you that you have chosen me and given me the same royal authority that Esther had. Help me, through my prayers and actions, bring divine transformation to the situations I face. In Jesus' name.

TRACY WILLIAMSON

Chosen to bring God's plans to birth

'Do not be afraid, Mary, you have found favour with God. You will conceive and give birth to a son, and you are to call him Jesus.'

Mary's story has an impact on us all. Only Mary could become Jesus' mother, but we are all chosen to carry the life of Christ and to bring God's purposes to birth.

Mary was a young woman like countless others. She lived with her family and was betrothed to Joseph. Her life seemed ordinary and mapped out, but Gabriel told her she had found special favour with God.

It is hard to believe that our holy God will look upon us with favour, but he sees beyond the outward things into our hearts. Every day we face choices—what we will focus upon, how we will react to situations, whether we will forgive or condemn, whether we will make time to listen to his voice. Our choices turn our hearts into storehouses of all that gives us character and depth. Worship of God and true acts of love all spring from this inner storehouse.

What was God searching for in the one he chose to nurture the life of his precious son? What he saw in her heart brought him great joy. Although so young, she was already nurturing a love for God. We see this through other glimpses into her story. For example, after the events of Jesus' conception and birth, Luke tells us, 'Mary treasured up all these things and pondered them in her heart' (2:19).

Treasuring God's words and ways are the key to fulfilling our God-given calling and living in his peace. God's choice of her meant that Mary faced rejection, misunderstanding, even the threat of death, yet her response was beautiful submission: '"I am the Lord's servant," Mary answered. "May your word to me be fulfilled"' (1:38).

We too are called to bring God's purposes to birth. Can we say 'yes' to him and daily treasure his life within us, as Mary did?

Dear Father, I desire to have a heart like Mary's, choosing to create a beautiful storehouse of worship and love. Forgive me for the times when I've ignored your voice. Please help me to keep saying 'yes' to you.

TRACY WILLIAMSON

Making links

Sandra Wheatley writes:

It's so often the case that the smallest words in scripture contain the greatest of treasures and often serve to open up a veritable storehouse for study and learning.

I usually pair 'mercy' with 'grace' and then have a delightful picture pop into my mind of two rotund, elderly aunts—'Auntie Grace and Auntie Mercy'—coming alongside to help me out each day.

Grace and mercy do sit alongside one another. It has been said that God's grace gives us the favour that we don't deserve, while his mercy holds back the judgement that we do deserve.

Mercy is mentioned hundreds of times in the Bible. Perhaps it is a very familiar idea to us, and yet we can't quite pin down exactly what it is or isn't.

Recently I heard Portia's speech from Shakespeare's *The Merchant of Venice* again. I was captivated and possibly understood it for the very first time. Portia speaks of mercy thus as she addresses Shylock:

The quality of mercy is not strain'd,
It droppeth as the gentle rain from heaven
Upon the place beneath: it is twice blest;
It blesseth him that gives and him that takes:
'Tis mightiest in the mightiest…
It is an attribute to God himself.
ACT IV, SCENE 1

When we receive mercy from the Lord and pass it to one another we really are 'twice blessed'. I hope this series of notes is a blessing received and then passed on to others.

Mercy experienced

He has shown you, O mortal, what is good. And what does the Lord require of you? To act justly and to love mercy and to walk humbly with your God.

Micah 6 seems to depict a courtroom setting, with God as the plaintiff, reminding his people of all he has done and of how much they have forgotten. Then he gives us the stripped-back simplicity of what he requires of us: 'to act justly and to love mercy and to walk humbly with your God'. This familiar verse sums up our Christian faith: be fair, be nice, be humble.

Just as grace can often sit alongside mercy, so too can justice, and it is often in a courtroom that mercy has an opportunity to be seen most clearly.

I've had little experience of being in court, thankfully, but I have often been in need of mercy rather than justice. I was recently 'invited' to attend a 'Drivers Awareness Course' after driving at 34mph in a 30mph area. I was amazed at how many others attended the course, but have been even more amazed at just how many of my friends have been to one too. No one likes to admit it!

The course wasn't in a judicial setting but the room was full of guilty people, like myself. Just for a moment, as the course started, I wondered whether the instructor could possibly say, 'You can all go home. You don't need to be here for four hours; you can go.' That would have been mercy in the face of justice. But he didn't. He had no reason to do so, and I actually learned a lot by being there, as well as avoiding three points on my licence.

Yet there is a place I've been, where my sin far outweighed any motoring offence. I needed more than a lesson: I needed forgiveness, grace, mercy, and a new start, a new life. At the cross I received all that and more.

Dear Lord, help me to act and love and walk as the scripture today encourages me to—justly, mercifully and humbly.

SANDRA WHEATLEY

Mercy seen

Jacob looked up and there was Esau, coming with his four hundred men.

When I approached this story, my sympathy veered from brother to brother, seeing things from Jacob's side, then from Esau's and back again. If you have time, it is well worth reading through the preceding chapters to this one. The story of Jacob and Esau resembles any modern-day TV soap.

As Jacob looked up, I'm sure he also looked back and recalled the last time he had seen his brother Esau and the final words he'd heard him speak: 'Isn't he rightly named Jacob? This is the second time he has taken advantage of me: he took my birthright, and now he's taken my blessing!' (Genesis 27:36) and 'I will kill my brother Jacob' (v. 41).

Twenty years had passed since Jacob fled—and now he was going home in great fear and distress (32:7), to face his brother and perhaps be torn limb from limb. It's a moment to hold our breath.

I've lost count of the times when I needed to face people I'd rather not face, to relive situations that needed resolution and reconciliation. None of us is immune from hurting or being hurt by those we love and who know us the best. Sometimes years pass, with the pain and the rifts getting deeper and wider, and the dread of meeting again grows and gnaws away at us. Yet I've never regretted taking that step and heading home—even in dread and distress.

I've tried to do as Jacob did—to meet with God beforehand, although not in the exact way that Jacob did! His encounter with God changed his name and life for ever (Genesis 32:22–30).

Jacob met Esau as a new man with a new name, as well as a limp—and amazingly he was met by a brother who didn't exact a terrible revenge but ran towards him, hugged him, kissed him and wept. No wonder Jacob said, 'To see your face is like seeing the face of God' (v. 10).

Jacob met with mercy. May our day today bring that same experience.
                                                            SANDRA WHEATLEY

Forever mercy

Oh, give thanks to the Lord, for He is good! For His mercy endures forever.

There is something very special about what you're holding and reading right now, not because of the contributors but because each day, as you read, there is an opportunity to meet with God through his word. This psalm is a fabulous example—especially as we read, 'His mercy endures forever' 26 times.

Psalm 136 is unique, as nowhere else in scripture is a stanza repeated so may times. There is something very helpful about repetition, especially of scripture. Each day has 24 hours and within each of those hours we have the chance to remind ourselves that 'his mercy endures forever', whatever we face.

Frances Ridley Havergal, author of the hymn 'Take my life and let it be…', wrote on her calendar every day at least one thing, no matter how small, for which she thanked God. Whatever our list of things to be thankful for, this psalm reminds us that, despite the 'daily-ness' of our lives, we have a 'forever mercy' in which to immerse ourselves.

Some years ago, I all but gave up on living. I faced eviction by a tyrant of a landlord; my health was deteriorating, the pain was incessant and my palliative care consultant was increasing my medication to levels that were creating a drug dependency I didn't want and a psychosis that terrified me. Morphine, methadone, ketamine—with each dose, I felt as if it was killing me. For the first time in my life, everything seemed futile. Then I read 2 Timothy 4:7, 'I have kept the faith'. I realised that 'faith' was all I had to cling to. Although I couldn't see how to get through each day, I decided that every hour, on the hour, I would whisper, 'I have kept the faith… I have kept the faith.' Gradually the feeling of futility left as I weaned myself off the medication and emerged into God's light again. Whatever you're facing today, his mercy endures and will hold you.

After this life, we have a glorious 'beyond', as his mercy endures forever. Thanks be to God.

SANDRA WHEATLEY

Mercy: cause and effect

'Blessed are the merciful, for they will be shown mercy.'

After almost 400 years of silence, the voice of God is heard again. After the prophecies of Malachi, there is no biblical record of God speaking directly with human beings until Jesus has been born. On this occasion, perhaps close to the beginning of his ministry, Jesus climbs to a vantage point on a hill and the waiting world hears, 'Blessed are…'. Within the sublime list of those who are blessed are 'the merciful'.

I think mercy was around before grace, as it took Jesus' death on the cross to usher us into this dispensation of grace. So to have these words of Jesus, as well as his parables about showing mercy (such as the good Samaritan in Luke 10:25–37 and the unforgiving servant in Matthew 18:21–35), is significant.

Jesus was the epitome of mercy: he walked it, lived it and showed it. Those who cried out for mercy were granted it and more, much more besides. The Gospels ooze with mercy. Even as Jesus is dying, his final few words, 'Father, forgive them, for they do not know what they are doing' (Luke 23:34), show us that mercy continues to flow from his lips to the very end.

Can I ever come anywhere near to being that merciful to others? I know I have received mercy upon mercy, when all I deserved from God was a good shaking! The challenge I face is to let that mercy flow freely, as Jesus did, rather than through gritted teeth and from a huffy heart. Jesus said that when we believe in him, 'rivers of living water will flow' from within us (John 7:38). Is mercy part of the sweetness within that stream? I need to let it flow, to let God pour in and then pour out those living, refreshing, merciful streams to touch the lives of all I meet today.

Lord Jesus, you poured out your life as an example for me to follow. Help me to do and be as you are—merciful and kind.

SANDRA WHEATLEY

A tale of two prayers

The tax collector stood at a distance. He would not even look up
to heaven, but beat his breast and said, 'God, have mercy on me,
a sinner.'

Within our reading today we can see both the best of prayers and the
worst of prayers.

Jesus told this story to an audience who viewed its main characters
very differently from the way we do. To us, because we're familiar with
the Gospels, the Pharisee is the 'baddie' and the tax collector the 'good
guy', but the people listening to Jesus would have respected the Pharisee and rejected the tax collector.

As I read this familiar story, it's a bit like looking at myself as if I
were two sides of the very same tarnished coin. I so easily slip into
'Pharisee' mode, comparing myself with others, deciding I'm doing OK
and patting myself on the back for my spiritual maturity and Christian walk. In the very next instant, though, I can be overwhelmed by
my own brokenness and deep need for mercy. I carry around an inner
Pharisee and tax collector every single day.

So often, even my prayers can be tinged with that air of 'Haven't I
done well, Lord…?' But more and more, the most effectual and honest of my prayers are the least eloquent, the shortest, the most needy:
'God, have mercy on me, a sinner.'

For a long time—too long—I entertained the notion that because
my sins were forgiven the moment I accepted Jesus as my Saviour, I no
longer 'sinned': the problem of sin in my life was dealt with 46 years
ago. I now know that this was wrong. Even today I need his mercy, and
I covet his grace and revel in his forgiveness.

'God, have mercy on me, a sinner' is the best of prayers for any of
us, for any day, for every day. Those seven short, simple and sincere
words are powerful words that move heaven and touch the heart of
God.

Father God, hear my prayer: have mercy on me a sinner. Amen

SANDRA WHEATLEY

Unexpected mercy

[Jesus asked] 'Which of these three do you think was a neighbour to the man who fell into the hands of robbers?' The expert in the law replied, 'The one who had mercy on him.'

I wondered whether or not to include this very well-known passage in our readings, not because it isn't absolutely spot-on as a perfect illustration for 'mercy' but because I sometimes feel overfamiliar with it. I can recite it verbatim, having heard it so often at church and Sunday school. I imagine I've heard every sermon about it, from every angle, and that there's nothing more to learn—but there always is.

I love to read scripture and imagine being part of it—in the crowd, in the boat, in the home or synagogue as Jesus teaches, speaks and heals—and I feel no different about the parable of the good Samaritan. Which character will I identify with? I hope it won't be the 'passing priest' or the 'looking Levite', but the hero—the good Samaritan. I'll go to the needy, the battered and bruised, and tend and care for them. I'll do what needs doing!

This time I read it, though, I'm the one battered and bruised, left for dead and overlooked by those I'd hoped would help me. This time it's me who is in need: I am to learn just who my neighbour is and to accept, from even the most unexpected and the most difficult of people, that they are the neighbours I am to love. That is what Jesus was saying in response to the question, 'Who is my neighbour?'

It is a shift in the way I understand the parable. For years I aspired to be the good Samaritan and took any opportunity to 'do likewise' in seeking out and helping those in need. But now I'm learning something new. Sometimes my needs have gone unnoticed by those whose help I expected. Instead, help comes in different places and from different people—some of whom have no faith, no Christian label at all. They are being, to me, the Samaritans I need to love, and I need to accept their kindness and mercy.

'Lord, who is my neighbour?'

SANDRA WHEATLEY

The triumph of mercy

Speak and act as those who are going to be judged by the law that gives freedom, because judgment without mercy will be shown to anyone who has not been merciful. Mercy triumphs over judgment.

In today's reading, James doesn't pull any punches in speaking about favouritism within the fledgling church. He likens it to any of the other sins mentioned in scripture and reminds the believers that if one aspect of the law is broken, then the entirety of it is broken. It's rather like seeing the law as a pane of glass instead of a list from which we can 'cherry-pick': if we break even the smallest of laws, we shatter the whole lot.

I am very conscious of how easy it is to break that glass—and relieved that God's grace and mercy are never diminished by my all-too-frequent need for them. The lesson for me is in realising that mercy received needs to become mercy given.

There's no better place than within our churches and fellowships to see these principles in action. Sadly, the situations described in James 2 can be re-enacted every Sunday we meet; church is a safe refuge for some, but for others it can be a minefield of criticism and disgruntlement over the smallest of issues. We forget mercy. I know I do. I forget that if I stand on my 'right' to do with others as I please—judging, ignoring, criticising—then God will stand on his right to judge me as I deserve. His justice will condemn—but his mercy and grace will forgive and redeem, and the cost of that redemption makes the mercy received all the more potent.

Justitia, Lady Justice, who stands high above the Old Bailey in London, is depicted as a woman with a sword in one hand, a set of scales in the other, and a conspicuous blindfold over her eyes. Could mercy be the same, without the scale and sword? Her hands open to all, blind to appearances, offering peace without prejudice? That is what I need to do and be.

Father God, please may your mercy continue to triumph in my life.

SANDRA WHEATLEY

Making links

Mary Reid writes:

Summer has gone: where I live, the farmers are working all hours, getting in the harvest. When I go into the garden in the evening, even when it is dark, I can still hear the distant sound of tractors and farm machinery hard at work.

September is a busy month, the beginning of a new academic year, with all our church activities starting up again after the summer break. It is a time of new beginnings, a time of change, so whether we are feeling low at the approach of winter or excited about the beginning of something new, we need to be reminded about what we are here for. What does God want us to achieve in our part of his world?

I was once grumbling about 'the state of the world', having read the daily newspaper over breakfast. Invariably the news was mostly bad, sad and very depressing. But then I was reminded by my daughter of something I had said to her when she was starting out in life: 'You can't change the whole world, but you can improve the part you live in.' It is all too easy to be discouraged and feel that Jesus is being ignored by most people. There are fewer people worshipping on Sundays: we now live in a secular society. But that means we have a real purpose in life—no matter how old or young we are. God has put us where we are for a purpose.

Paul's letter to the Ephesians gives us answers to the questions we may be asking, answers that give us hope for the present and for the future.

Keeping in touch

May God our Father and the Lord Jesus Christ give you grace and peace.

I have just replaced my old mobile phone for a smartphone so I can text my family—and maybe even work out how to send emails and photos to them, as they do to me.

I am trying to catch up with today's ways of communicating, but I still prefer old-fashioned letters. As I write these notes, I have by my desk a whole box of Christmas letters waiting to be read and re-read. I keep them for the whole year; they refresh my memory of old friends and their growing families. They are a source of thanks for good times past and a reminder of those who need my prayers.

Paul's letters to the young churches are full of wisdom and inspiration—not only to the people who received them so many years ago, but to us as we read them today. His letter to the Ephesians was written to help that young church see a wider picture of God's plan, to help them understand the purpose he had for them and to remind them of the eternal grace and peace that was available to all who love him.

As Paul writes about God's grace and peace, both he and Timothy are in prison in Rome. He writes about being an apostle 'by God's will'. So was it God's will that he and Timothy should be in prison with little prospect of regaining freedom?

Even in that situation, Paul sees purpose in his very restricted life. It means he has time to write letters of encouragement, wisdom and advice to the churches he was once able to be with in person. He knows the difficulties they face. He prays for them, and he can write them letters—letters that we can read and learn from 2000 years later.

Is there someone you haven't contacted for a long time who would enjoy a phone call or a letter from you? Pray for them today.

MARY REID

Chosen by God

Even before the world was made, God had already chosen us to be his through our union with Christ.

I still remember what it felt like, waiting to be chosen to play in a rounders team, way back in my schooldays—trying not to look anxious, not wanting to be left until last. I can still fee the dread of not being chosen at all.

There are plenty of occasions in life when we have to wait to be chosen—when applying for a job, for example—but mostly in our Western society we are the choosers. We choose what to wear; we choose where to go on holiday (if we are lucky enough to be able to afford a holiday); we choose what to buy every time we go to the supermarket. We just assume that we make all the decisions and choices in our everyday lives.

As Christians, we made the most important choice of all when we decided to accept Jesus as our Saviour and friend, yet here Paul says that we were chosen by God even before the world was made. Does this mean that we don't need to pray for the conversion of those who haven't yet chosen to be followers of Jesus because God has already chosen those he wants to be his children?

We need to remember that God wants everyone to be part of his perfect creation (see 2 Peter 3:9). It is often difficult to accept this fact when we read of atrocities committed by human beings against other human beings. Surely God hasn't chosen people like that to be his children? Yet that is what this seems to say: God chose everyone. But Paul says more: 'God had already chosen us... through our union with Christ.' So it is through our belief in Jesus, his Son, that God's choice of us is made complete.

We are not only chosen but given a work to do (see John 15:16–17).

MARY REID

God's great plan

For by the sacrificial death of Christ we are set free, that is, our sins are forgiven.

One of my earliest memories is of sitting curled up in a favourite arm-chair looking at a very large old-fashioned book I had taken out of the bookcase beside me. Published in the late 1800s, it was intended for 'suitable Sunday reading'. On the page in front of me was a graphic picture of the crucifixion. I wept over that picture. As a child, I could not understand why the gentle Jesus to whom I said my prayers every evening had to die.

These few verses in Ephesians spell out why Jesus died. It was God's plan that through the death of Christ we should be freed from the penalty of our sinfulness. Now, God sees us as perfect instead of imperfect. All our sins—past, present and future—are blotted out. We are redeemed and forgiven and adopted into his family.

Paul echoes the story of the Passover, when, through the blood of the lamb, the children of Israel were saved from death. They were then freed from slavery in Egypt and began their journey to the promised land (Exodus 12). We are also on a journey to our 'promised land', and we need to live our lives in the light of eternity—that time when 'everything in heaven and on earth' comes together with Christ as head (v. 10).

In the meantime, we have been given grace in 'large measure' (vv. 7–8) to live our everyday lives as his representatives, in spite of all the complications and sadnesses of our 21st-century world. We know we are part of God's great plan, and there is plenty of work for us to do, reflecting the love and care of Jesus to those around us.

Read Colossians 1:15–20 and give thanks for Jesus.

MARY REID

Our heavenly inheritance

The Spirit is the guarantee that we shall receive what God has promised his people.

Paul makes it quite clear, in this letter to the church in Ephesus, that God chose not only Jews but also Gentiles to be his people. Today, the church is worldwide: people of practically every race and nationality have become God's people.

Paul writes that God 'chose us to be his own people' (v. 11), and in verse 13 he adds, 'You also became God's people when you heard the true message.' Because we are God's people, whenever we meet other Christians (not necessarily in church) we quickly recognise that we have something in common. We have the gift of his Spirit. God has put his 'stamp of ownership' on us.

I first became aware of this recognition of other Christians when I was emigrating to Canada, many years ago. As a somewhat shy English person on a ship full of strangers, I found myself eating supper next to a Canadian couple. I immediately felt drawn to them. Within five minutes I realised that they too were Christians.

Paul points out that 'the Spirit is the guarantee that we shall receive what God has promised' (v. 14). The Greek word translated here as 'guarantee' was a commercial term meaning 'down-payment', the first instalment when buying something. Our experience of the Holy Spirit is God's down-payment, his guarantee that we will receive what he has promised us in full (see 2 Corinthians 5:5).

We have the joy now of being part of a worldwide family, with the assurance of knowing that we have a great inheritance to look forward to.

Thank you, Father, for calling me to be part of your family and for sending your Spirit to be with me every day of my life.

MARY REID

Praying for you

I have not stopped giving thanks to God for you. I remember you in my prayers and ask the God of our Lord Jesus Christ, the glorious Father, to give you the Spirit, who will make you wise and reveal God to you, so that you will know him.

News has got through to Paul about the growth of the church in Ephesus, and although no one is mentioned by name in this letter, the news is good. His response, as well as to write, is to pray—and to pray intelligently.

These few verses give us guidelines for our own prayers. We also need to know who we are praying for, to be able to give thanks to God for them; we can then pray for their needs. In this example Paul is praying that the Ephesians will have the Spirit, who will give them wisdom and insight. He asks for their minds to be opened so that they may know the hope and blessings they have received (v. 18). Clearly their faith is not based on emotions—the way they feel. Paul prays for their faith to be based on what they know, facts rather than feelings. So often I have heard of young Christians struggling because they no longer felt the excitement and delight of their conversion. We all have periods when we don't feel God around us. It is at these times that we need to 'know' the hope we have.

Faith and love (v. 15) are basic Christian graces. I used to accompany my husband to many church services in the diocese in which he worked. Occasionally, on entering a church, I would sense that the people sitting in the pews didn't even like each other, let alone love each other. Fortunately it wasn't often like that. In other churches there was a real buzz before the service began. People would be walking around, greeting each other, smiling and sharing news. As a stranger I would be quickly noticed and welcomed. Was this like the Ephesian church that Paul was giving thanks for? I think so.

Is there anyone in your church who may be feeling a little unloved? Make sure he or she is included and cared for next time you meet for worship.

MARY REID

We are his body

The church is Christ's body, the completion of him who himself completes all things everywhere.

Paul has already written about the gifts of wisdom and insight that are available to those who have been given the Spirit. In today's verses we read that the power that raised Jesus from death and set him to rule above everything is the same power at work in us (vv. 19–20). How amazing! Yet even more amazing is the fact that, as small and insignificant as we may feel, we really do have this power.

Most of the time, we accept that we have been given his Spirit, but we don't necessarily feel mighty and powerful. Many years ago, when I was attending a confirmation class, the vicar gave a very good story to illustrate the gift of the Spirit to us. 'You have been given,' he said, 'a train ticket to London, which you have accepted gratefully. You put it safely away in your wallet, and there it stays. It is not until you actually use it and get on the train that you find out what it can do.'

Do most of us keep the Holy Spirit safely tucked away, unaware of the strength and power that are available to us? How often do we shrink away from accepting a new challenge in our lives—moving to a new job away from home, or helping to run a youth group, for example? It is when we accept a new challenge that we become aware of the strength the Spirit gives us.

Paul goes on to point out that we, the church, are Christ's body. We are his hands and feet. People can only see Jesus when we see ourselves as 'Jesus in this place'—our home, our job, our neighbourhood. Wherever we are, whatever role or job we do, we are there for a purpose—to be Christ's body in that place.

Over the next few days or weeks, read through Mark's Gospel and note what Jesus says, what he does, how he relates to people—and see how they want to be near him.

MARY REID

We have purpose

God has made us what we are, and in our union with Christ Jesus he has created us for a life of good deeds, which he has already prepared for us to do.

These seven verses set out clearly the new life we have in Christ. Twice Paul writes, 'It is by God's grace that you have been saved' (vv. 5, 8). Whenever we say the Apostles' Creed, we remind ourselves of the fact that Jesus rose from the dead, ascended into heaven and sits with God the Father. Here Paul is pointing out that 'in our union with Christ Jesus he raised us up with him… in the heavenly world' (v. 6). We are already part of his kingdom in heaven, even though we are still on earth.

I once tried to draw what it was like to live as a Christian in our fallen world, showing how stressful it can be to live in a world where there is so much going wrong all the time. My picture of plants being stretched between earth and heaven ended up in the wastepaper basket—but it is in exactly this stressful situation that we have a work to do. We may not be able to change the whole world, but 'God has made us what we are' and he has 'created us for a life of good deeds, which he has already prepared for us to do' (v. 10).

I need to have this verse pinned up by my desk, in the kitchen, or anywhere, as a constant reminder that God intends me to be where I am and that there is work to do here as a member of his kingdom on earth. As an ex-teacher and ex-editor, I often note errors in books. I have found one in my version of the GNB in this verse. It has the words 'already prepared for us to do' printed twice. Perhaps it's not an error but a double reminder!

Look up Jeremiah 29:11 and thank God for his promise.

MARY REID

Peace to all

So Christ came and preached the Good News of peace to all... It is through Christ that all of us, Jews and Gentiles, are able to come in the one Spirit into the presence of the Father.

I enjoy singing carols at Christmas but the words in 'It came upon the midnight clear'—'peace on the earth, goodwill to men'—leave me feeling very wistful. Paul's letter was written to a church made up of Jews and Gentiles who, until the growth of the Christian church, had hated each other. He writes that it was through Christ that they were able to come together to worship God. So why is it that in the 21st century we Christians don't always live with goodwill to one another?

Paul gives us two pictures of the church—as a family and as a building. 'You are now... members of the family of God. You, too, are built upon the foundation laid by the apostles and prophets, the cornerstone being Christ Jesus himself' (vv. 19–20). I am certainly not an architect, but the importance of a sound foundation seems obvious to me. Paul likens these sound foundations to sound teachings—for us, the good news of the gospel—but the cornerstone is even more vital. It is the stone at the apex of the building, which keeps all the other stones standing. Without the cornerstone the building would collapse. Our cornerstone is Christ Jesus.

The Christian church today is made up of many different denominations and different nationalities. How do we cope with the arguments and disagreements that, if we're honest, we see in our own churches? Perhaps this is where Paul's other picture of the church, as a 'family', fits in. Have you ever noted how children in the same family squabble and bicker over unimportant things—yet when they are in real trouble they cling together in unity?

The church today always gets publicity when it has disagreements, but will the pressure of our increasingly secular society bring us together in unity?

Dear Father, forgive us when we feel at odds with others in our Christian family. Help us to focus on Jesus as our cornerstone, and give us your peace. Amen

MARY REID

The power of prayer

I pray that Christ will make his home in your hearts through faith.

Throughout this letter, Paul mixes advice and information with prayer. His prayer is for the young churches that he has taken part in leading: he knows their needs, and now that he is in prison he constantly prays for them.

I once went on a holiday that promised we would be 'following in the steps of St Paul'. For the first time I realised the vast distances that Paul travelled as he went from one church to another with the good news of Jesus. Some of his journeys would have been by sea, in a small sailing ship. On land he would have walked for miles. Our ability to cover the same distances in comfort and at speed made me contemplate what it must have been like for Paul.

I am sure he didn't wait until he arrived at a church along the way before he prayed. Prayer would have been, for him, a constant communion with God. All those miles of walking would have given him space and time for praying.

Life for our present-day missionaries is very different. They don't have to walk miles. Communication via the internet is possible, wherever in the world they are working, but they still communicate with our heavenly Father by prayer, and we need to support them constantly through our prayers.

My husband was once taken to visit an elderly woman who was housebound. Much to his surprise, on entering the house, his companion called out to her, 'Where are you today, Vera?' 'South America,' came the reply. Laid out on the kitchen table was prayer literature for mission agencies working in South America. Housebound she may have been, but what a ministry of prayer she had!

Do you support a particular Christian working overseas? Spend time catching up on their needs and ask for God's blessing on their work.

MARY REID

God's standards

Live a life that measures up to the standard God set when he called you. Be always humble, gentle, and patient. Show your love by being tolerant with one another.

I once needed a day off work, so I arranged for a friend to take over my dinner-lady duty. The next day I discovered that the other dinner-ladies were furious with me, as they thought I should have just taken the day off 'sick', which is what they always did. God's standards are not the same as the world's standards, as I discovered there to my cost.

Paul tells us 'to live a life that measures up to the standard God set' when we were called to follow Jesus. We have been told that the church is his body (1:23): we are his representatives in today's Western world. We have to measure ourselves against Jesus. What is now counted as a perfectly acceptable way to behave is not always God's way, so we need to be aware that we can gradually slip away from the standards we set ourselves when we first became Christians.

The qualities Paul lists here seem very meek and mild, and perhaps even weak—humility, gentleness, patience, tolerance and love. In fact, though, they are quite the opposite: they are the qualities that are usually seen in a strong person. For example, let's consider 'humility'. The church I belonged to as a teenager had an eminent Christian leader in the congregation, someone I greatly admired. He always found something helpful and encouraging in the sermons preached by either our vicar or our curate. For me, that was a demonstration of Christian humility.

All these qualities are an expression of Christian love. The Greek word for 'love' used here is *agape*—a love that is nothing to do with emotion but all to do with our will. Next time you are really irritated by someone going on and on about the government or some other bugbear, exercise patience and tolerance. You are the body of Christ.

Thank you, Father, for calling me to be your child. Help me to show these qualities today.

MARY REID

United we stand

Do your best to preserve the unity which the Spirit gives by means of the peace that binds you together.

The qualities of Christian love that we thought about yesterday are the foundation stones of unity. Paul now points out that there is one body, one Spirit, one hope, one Lord, one faith, one baptism, one God and Father of all humankind. With all these factors that make us one body, why do we have so many different church groups and denominations—and, sadly, divisions? We have already read that the church is Christ's body in the world, so is his body divided?

I used to work in the advertising department of a large international company selling soap powders. The company made several different brands of powder, all designed to make laundered clothes whiter and brighter. This puzzled me at first: why not concentrate on just one brand? 'Ah,' I was told, 'more brands get more shelf space for us in the supermarkets!'

If the church is divided into many different denominations does this mean that we have the equivalent of more shelf space in our communities?

I live in a small but lively market town. On Good Friday we have a Walk of Witness. A motley crowd gathers at the starting place, coming from all the local churches—Anglican, Methodist, URC, Baptist, Roman Catholic, house church and Quakers. We all have different styles of worship, but all are united in Christ as Lord and Saviour.

When we get together for the Good Friday event, it is quite impressive. A large wooden cross is carried at the head of the procession and we all follow, reverently silent, holding up the traffic along the way. People out shopping may stop to watch or pretend they haven't noticed us. But we are all, I am sure, wanting our town to see that we are united in our faith in the crucified and risen Lord.

Is there any way the churches work together to be the body of Christ in your part of the world? If so, do you support this work?

MARY REID

Using our gifts

Each one of us has received a special gift in proportion to what Christ has given... He did this to prepare all God's people for the work of Christian service, in order to build up the body of Christ.

Have you ever watched small children open their Christmas gifts? There is excitement as they tear off the wrapping paper, and once they have discovered the toy inside, they start playing with it straight away. We don't expect them to sit and look at it—or, worse, just put it away in the toy cupboard. But is this what some of us do with our gifts? Perhaps the gift we have been given isn't really the gift we wanted (and here I am not talking about Christmas presents).

Paul gives another of his lists in verse 11: Christ has appointed apostles, prophets, evangelists, pastors and teachers. When Paul wrote it, those were the gifts that the young church in Ephesus needed. We still need people with these gifts today, but it doesn't mean that more ordinary gifts aren't important too. Each one of us has received a special gift, and we need to know what our gift is in order to exercise it—to use it both within our church fellowship and in our community, remembering that we are the body of Christ.

Maybe your gift is being a good organiser, or showing hospitality to your neighbours, or having the gift of caring for others.

Someone I know had a marvellous singing voice and was learning to play the guitar. He was a perfectionist, and every day he took himself off to a distant room in the house, closed the door and practised. No one was allowed to listen—not until he was as good as Segovia! Eventually an exasperated member of the family told him to share his gift, not hide it away: he didn't have to wait until he was 100 per cent perfect. He began to use his gift both in church and in village gatherings, giving honour to God and blessing to others.

Are you hiding your gifts and abilities because you feel they are not good enough to be of use? Be brave and find out how you can use your God-given gifts in Christian service.

MARY REID

33

Growing up

We shall all come together to that oneness in our faith and in our knowledge of the Son of God; we shall become mature people, reaching to the very height of Christ's full stature.

Have you ever been tempted to tell someone to 'grow up and stop being so childish'? We all expect adults to behave like adults, but it doesn't always happen. Even though you may have been too polite to say those words, I am sure there have been times when you have thought them.

Anyone who has only just become a Christian is vulnerable to the clever arguments of those who are against Christianity. It is very hard for a young Christian (in years as well as in faith) to stand up to peer pressure against belonging to a church fellowship. The picture here of 'children carried by the waves and blown about by every shifting wind' (v. 14) emphasises how important it is that we help them become mature in their faith.

Paul says that we need to come together in 'oneness' (v. 13): other translations of the Bible use the word 'unity'. As the church is the body of Christ, every part of it needs to work together in harmony. When Christians disagree or fall out with each other, the whole body is harmed.

I once damaged the sciatic nerve in my leg. I was in considerable pain; not only was I unable to walk very far, but I even needed a stick to help me stand, and that meant my hands were out of action too. Because of the injury to one part, it seemed that my whole body was out of action.

As the body of Christ in our world, we cannot afford to have any part of the church out of action. We need to be fit and in good working order, mature in our faith and living in unity with each other.

Pray for any new Christians you know in your church fellowship, that they will quickly reach maturity in their faith.

MARY REID

Living love

Since you are God's dear children, you must try to be like him. Your life must be controlled by love, just as Christ loved us and gave his life for us as a sweet-smelling offering and sacrifice that pleases God.

Looking at my old family photos can be quite entertaining—especially sorting through really old sepia snaps taken by my parents when they were young. In some you can see a family likeness that has been passed on to our children and grandchildren.

Photos, though, don't tell you anything about the temperament of a person, just what they look like. Our passage today is all about being like our heavenly Father. We are his children—and it says we must *try* to be like him. This isn't something that happens without any effort on our part. Becoming Christians doesn't automatically make us loving and kind people, especially if, until that point in our lives, we have been quite self-centred—but we have become his children.

Children imitate those closest to them. A baby born into a truly loving family is cared for and loved from the very beginning. Right through from the time of broken nights as a baby to the complications of teenage years, the child is loved and is part of the family, but in the growing years that child has to learn how to behave. It is just like this when we become part of God's family.

We have to know Jesus if we are to be like him. We need to immerse ourselves in the stories of Jesus in the Gospels, noting how he dealt with Zacchaeus the tax collector, how he cared for the sick and lame, and his patience with the disciples when they didn't always understand what he was saying. What an amazing example of love in action—and we must try to be like him. We will need to keep working on this, and it may take some time, but we are secure in the knowledge that we are part of God's family.

Look up these references on love: John 15:12; 1 Corinthians 13:4–7; Colossians 3:14 and 1 John 4:19. Let Jesus' love transform you so that you can show his love to others.

MARY REID

Making links

Rosemary Green writes:

'It's a man's world!' That is how we might often think of the early church. The major characters in the book of Acts are indeed men: Peter and Paul are the lead characters, with a strong and varied supporting cast, largely male. There are women as well, however, some of whom played significant parts and others whom we might easily pass over. For these studies on the women in the book of Acts, I originally selected those who were more noticeable, but then I was asked to write a fortnight's worth of notes. It has been good to peruse the book more closely and to notice some of the women I had overlooked, who are mentioned only briefly, some not even named. These women had different gifts and played different roles. They came from various countries round the Mediterranean and belonged to a variety of social strata. Some of their lives are warnings for us rather than examples to follow, but all, even the apparently least noticeable, have something to teach us about the sort of people we are, the way we live and serve.

One thing that strikes me is that, in contrast with many women today, they appear to be content with their status. I appreciate that women today command more respect than they have done in times past, and that is thanks in great part to those like the suffragettes and others who have fought for women's rights, but there can also be strength in being content to be in the background, not always fighting militantly for new status. Faithful, reliable, loving service is commended by God as much as strident leadership. I hope that we each strive more for change in our characters than for change in our status. Paul wrote from an uncomfortable prison, 'I have learned to be content whatever the circumstances' (Philippians 4:11). Let us strive for similar contentment.

Faithfulness

When [the apostles] arrived, they went upstairs to the room where they were staying. Those present [included] Peter, John, James and Andrew… They all joined together constantly in prayer, along with the women and Mary the mother of Jesus, and his brothers.

The inner core of Jesus' followers had their last sight of him on a small hill outside Jerusalem. Before he ascended, he told them to stay in Jerusalem to wait for the Holy Spirit who would empower them as his witnesses. They returned to the city full of joy. Their expectancy about the future (though unknown) overcame their sadness at his final departure.

The group included the Eleven (twelve minus Judas), Jesus' mother and—a huge surprise—his brothers, previously among his biggest sceptics. There were also 'the women'. As Luke starts Part 2 of Luke–Acts, he is referring to the women who had followed Jesus from Galilee. He first mentions them in Luke 8:2–3, travelling with Jesus and his disciples, 'helping to support them out of their own means'. I am struck by their faithfulness, their generosity and their quiet service. They were there when Jesus hung on the cross. After his death they prepared the spices to embalm his body, and as early as possible after the sabbath they went to the tomb. Imagine their shock to find the stone rolled back, the gaping hole, the empty tomb—and then the angels with their message of God's purposes and Jesus risen! No wonder their excitement overflowed as they ran back to the other disciples. There, they received the rebuff of disbelief, but they knew what they had seen and heard.

As we seek to share the good news of Jesus some will scoff, others will be apathetic, and a few interested, but we can stick to our story—the truth of his story and of our own experience. May we, like these women, be faithful in our witness as well as in our simple service.

What charactistic of these women most challenges you? Their generosity? Their quiet dedication? Their selfless service? Their prayerfulness? Their excitement in sharing the news of the empty tomb and the risen Jesus?

Lord, I pray that I may follow their example.

ROSEMARY GREEN

A meditative woman

When the wine was gone, Jesus' mother said to him, 'They have
no more wine.' 'Woman, why do you involve me?' Jesus replied.
'My hour has not yet come.' His mother said to the servants, 'Do
whatever he tells you.'

Mary, Jesus' mother, is the one woman in the group whom Luke names,
so today we stray from our readings in Acts to focus on her. We are very
familiar with the Christmas story, and the Magnificat shows something
of Mary's trust in God (Luke 1:46–55), but what about other glimpses
of her?

She was deeply thoughtful: 'Mary treasured all these things in her
heart' (Luke 2:19, 51). We read this after the shepherds have left; we
read it again when the twelve-year-old Jesus asks his parents, 'Didn't
you know I had to be in my Father's house?' The adults didn't understand at the time, but Mary thought deeply about it all. In the pace of
our daily lives, we do not always stop to meditate, to 'ponder'.

Mary had courage. She saw that Jesus was unique and she played
a significant part in his first public miracle. She approached him with
news of the shortage of wine, and, despite his apparent rebuff, spoke in
faith to the servants: 'Do whatever he tells you.'

Did her faith wobble under the influence of her sceptical sons? She
was with them when they called Jesus insane and tried to get him out of
the public eye (Mark 3:21), but a temporary glitch in our faith does not
spell disaster. Doubt may lead us to think more deeply about our faith
and, ultimately, to build a faith more secure than it was before.

Some people think that Salome, mother of James and John, may
have been Mary's sister. Whether or not that is so, it was to John, not
to his own brothers, that Jesus committed Mary's care as he died (John
19:26–27). This tells me there was a close relationship between Mary
and John—two thoughtful, insightful people.

Lord, I pray that I may grow in contemplation, like Mary.

ROSEMARY GREEN

A diverse group

The twelve were with him, as well as some women who had been cured of evil spirits and infirmities: Mary, called Magdalene, from whom seven demons had gone out, and Joanna, the wife of Herod's steward Chuza, and Susanna, and many others, who provided for them out of their resources.

As a child, I used to enjoy treasure hunts (I still enjoy playing hide-and-seek with my grandchildren) and I find it fascinating to hunt through the Gospels to find out more about the mixed group of women who were with the disciples in the upper room. Yesterday just one woman, Mary the mother of Jesus, was named. Today we think about some of the others.

This group of women, probably the same women mentioned in Acts 1:14, were very varied in their backgrounds. Mary Magdalene, the ex-prostitute, had been released from bondage to demons. She is probably the woman who anointed Jesus' feet with expensive ointment: she was lavish with her love, deeply grateful for what he had done for her. Joanna, the wife of Herod's household manager (I think of the butler in *Downton Abbey*!), was probably used to mixing in high society. Of Susanna I know nothing. Mentioned elsewhere with this group was Salome, the mother of James and John, who was married to Zebedee, a fisherman. Mary, wife of Alphaeus, was the mother of James (another member of the Twelve) and Joses. Paul wrote in Galatians 3:28, 'There is no longer Jew or Greek, there is no longer slave or free, there is no longer male and female; for all of you are one in Christ Jesus.' Christian fellowship embraces all of us, equally.

What about the backgrounds of our friends? If the spectrum of age, nationality or social standing is limited, perhaps we could think about how we might widen the circle. That will widen our own perspectives and demonstrate the reality of Jesus for all people.

Lord, I pray for a new love for those who come from very different backgrounds from my own, and for new ease in relating to them.

ROSEMARY GREEN

Truth matters

Now a man named Ananias, together with his wife Sapphira, also sold a piece of property. With his wife's full knowledge he kept back part of the money for himself, but brought the rest and put it at the apostles' feet.

The church in Jerusalem was flourishing. One strong mark of their vibrancy was their concern for the poor and the way they sat loose to their possessions. I often cling to unnecessary belongings. After all, 'they might come in useful some day' (even if they're left unused for a decade).

Ananias and Sapphira had seen Barnabas sell a field and give the money away. Imagine their conversation: 'Ought we to do that?' 'Perhaps, but...' They get a Brownie point for sharing their financial decisions—it's not so in many marriages—but, sadly, they also shared the decision to deceive. Peter was clearly given a spiritual gift of insight (Paul calls it 'a message of knowledge' in 1 Corinthians 12:8), although he may also have noticed something shifty in Ananias' attitude. Peter's questions were clear and decisive. He didn't mind that Ananias had brought only part of the money, but he did mind about the deceit. 'You have not lied just to human beings but to God' (v. 4). The shock of exposure for Ananias appears to have induced a massive heart attack.

Three hours later, enter Sapphira. Peter's apparently open question ('Is that the price?') leads her into confirming the lie. Again, Peter is concerned that her deceit is against God. In some ways that is nonsense. We cannot possibly hide from him, as Adam found in the garden of Eden. But this story brings home to me hard the sin of my supposedly 'little deceits'. They matter. They matter to God. Hebrews 10:31 comes to mind. 'It is a dreadful thing to fall into the hands of the living God.' God's love for us is not wishy-washy. His love is concerned for our best. My love for him should motivate me to please him in everything.

Ananias and Sapphira were motivated by greed. Ask yourself, 'What motivates any ungodliness in my life?'

Lord, I pray for your Holy Spirit to wash me through and through as I repent of my sin and deceit and seek to change.

ROSEMARY GREEN

Love in action

In Joppa there was a disciple named [Dorcas]; she was always doing good and helping the poor. About that time she became ill and died, and her body was washed and placed in an upstairs room... All the widows stood around [Peter], crying and showing him the robes and other clothing Dorcas had made them while she was still with them.

We could focus today on the striking example of God's power in action—one of only two occasions in the book of Acts when we see someone raised from the dead. Peter followed the example of Jesus with Jairus' daughter: he excluded the crowd, took Dorcas's hand and told her to get up (Luke 8:51–55).

Our focus, however, is on God's love in action. Dorcas shows a lovely example of practical care and love (in keeping with the not-yet-written 1 Timothy 5:10). I imagine she kept pretty busy. At home, she was constantly sewing (in the evening, by the feeble light of a small oil lamp) or entertaining lonely guests. Out and about, she visited needy widows, took them gifts and just showed that she cared. Their tears when she died were more for the loss of a loving friend than for their clothes.

Our church runs a monthly coffee morning for bereaved and other lonely people. We try to do it nicely, with colourful tablecloths, flowers, homemade food, a friendly welcome and a short talk on a Bible verse. As important as the coffee morning itself is visiting people at home between times, showing that we care about individuals—a pale reflection of God's love and care.

Very different is the love shown by a couple we know whose great concern is for widows in Zimbabwe. Often these are white women, stripped of farms and livelihood, living on tiny pensions whose value has been eroded by astronomical inflation. Among other ways of raising support, this couple's long-distance sponsored walks (the latest, from York to Canterbury) have raised millions of pounds. Again, I see love in action.

We own a picture from Haiti of a parent bird feeding her chicks, entitled 'Love is an active verb'. How do you show God's love in action?

ROSEMARY GREEN

Hospitality

Peter came to himself and said, 'Now I know without a doubt
that the Lord has sent his angel and rescued me…' When this had
dawned on him, he went to the house of Mary the mother of John,
also called Mark, where many people had gathered and were
praying.

Are angels real? Do they still appear nowadays? Yes! I have not consciously seen an angel myself, but I have heard enough first-hand stories to convince me of their activity today. Even Peter thought at first
that he was seeing a vision; he only recognised the angel's reality when
he was on the hard street and the angel disappeared.

He had no doubt about where to go to find his friends. I often wonder whether the upper room of the Last Supper, the upstairs room of
the first prayer meeting after Jesus ascended and the place where they
gathered on the Day of Pentecost were one and the same, in Mary's
home. I don't want to make 2 plus 2 equal 5, but it seems likely. If so,
this was the Christians' main base for their meetings (and, for some,
their residence). That would say a lot about Mary, although this is the
only time she is named. She was closely related to Barnabas, a well-off
landowner who was already a trusted leader in the Jerusalem church.
However spacious the house, however many servants, there were
demands on Mary and her hospitality. I wonder whether I would have
been as welcoming.

Peter and Paul both tell us to be hospitable. An individual for a
cuppa, a group for a meal—I find those easy to welcome, but resident
guests, apart from close family, are much harder. Peter's injunction to
'offer hospitality to one another without grumbling' (1 Peter 4:9) is set
in the context of telling us to use whatever gifts we have received to
serve others. Some are clearly given a special gift of hospitality. Mary
was; I'm not—and I have to find my right level of being hospitable, not
feeling guilty when I don't match up to others.

---

*'An Englishwoman's home is her castle.' If yours is, think and pray about
how you might let down the drawbridge and make it a place of welcome.*
ROSEMARY GREEN

She stuck to her story

When [Peter] knocked at the outer gate, a maid named Rhoda
came to answer. On recognising Peter's voice, she was so
overjoyed that, instead of opening the gate, she ran in and
announced that Peter was standing at the gate. They said to her,
'You are out of your mind!' But she insisted that it was so. They said,
'It is his angel.'

They were praying fervently, 'Lord, please keep him safe... Lord, rescue
him... Lord, surely you don't want Peter killed as well as James.' But
did they expect their prayers to be answered? Apparently not! We might
reflect on our own intercession and on our level of expectation for God
to answer prayer in his own way and in his own time, not according to
our plans.

Mary and Rhoda were at opposite ends of the social scale, and
Rhoda probably felt herself to be an insignificant underdog. It was her
role to leave the prayer meeting to answer the door. Her joy at hearing
Peter's voice overcame her common sense, and he was left standing
outside while she rushed in with the news. 'You're crazy! You're imagin-
ing it!' 'No, it's true.' Servant though she was, she stuck to her story.
They were still astonished when they opened the gate to his persistent
knocking. Yes, her story was true.

I like this story as an illustration of our testimony to our not-yet-
Christian friends about our faith. Rhoda didn't know much; she had
only heard Peter's voice, not even seen him outside. Yet she told what
she knew: 'I heard his voice.' She persevered until the others investi-
gated for themselves. Even if I feel I don't know much and cannot rebut
my friends' scepticism, they may eventually investigate for themselves
and come to believe, if I stick to my story. May I pray for them with
greater expectancy than this group did for Peter!

'Tell this to James,' said Peter. The James of the Gospels was dead
(Acts 12:2), but Jesus' brother James was a leader in the church in Jerusalem (15:13).

---

*Lord, I pray that I may be bold to talk more about you in this secular,
unbelieving climate. May I know when and how to speak and when to
be silent.*

ROSEMARY GREEN

Parenting and grandparenting

Paul came to Derbe and then to Lystra, where a disciple named
Timothy lived, whose mother was Jewish and a believer but whose
father was a Greek. The believers at Lystra and Iconium spoke well
of him.

Paul saw potential in the young man Timothy and decided to take him
along as an apprentice. Timothy's growth in responsibility over the
years, being eventually left in charge of the church in Ephesus, justi-
fies Paul's early assessment of him. His father was not, apparently, a
believer—a situation only too common in many homes today—but this
did not deter the women of the family. Even before his grandmother Lois
and his mother Eunice had become Christians, they laid a good foundation for Timothy's faith, teaching him the Old Testament from an early
age (2 Timothy 3:14–15). When our children were young, the bedtime
Bible story was always a fun feature. I think it is criminal when we communicate that Christianity is dull. When our young grandchildren come
to stay, we usually tell them a Bible story before bed (sometimes accompanied by the stick-men drawings we used with our own children).
   We often consider the challenges of being a parent, but what advice
is offered to grandparents? I recently led a church seminar on the question 'How can I cope with being a grandparent?' Being a grandparent
is a great privilege—and with privilege always comes responsibility.
Grandparental responsibilities vary enormously. Some have daily care
while parents are out; for others, distance or strained relationships
mean that grandchildren are rarely seen. Phone calls, letters and time
together can all help to develop a special relationship with our grandchildren, even if things are difficult with their parents. This special
relationship is most easily fostered when even the best of parents are
absent—but never forget that they are the parents' children before they
are our grandchildren.
   If you have no children or grandchildren of your own, are there any
children you could 'adopt' (informally!) to make them feel special?

---

*Father, thank you for the privilege of giving us children whom we can
love, pray for and influence for you.*

ROSEMARY GREEN

Open heart, open home

One of those listening was a woman from the city of Thyatira named Lydia, a dealer in purple cloth. She was a worshipper of God. The Lord opened her heart to respond to Paul's message. When she and the members of her household were baptised, she invited us to her home.

Thirty years ago, when visiting a town in the Midlands, I started to talk with a young woman serving in the sweet shop and invited her to church. When I found her name was Lydia, I told her about her namesake who 'opened her heart to respond' to Jesus. I didn't see her again but I still pray for her occasionally.

The Lydia we read about today was a businesswoman, a dealer in textiles. She came from Thyatira, a town near Ephesus, in western Turkey. Luke describes her as 'a worshipper of God'—one from another nation who believed in the God of Israel; she was already a regular participant in the sabbath time of prayer. As Paul spoke to the group about Jesus, she was more than ready to open her heart to his Spirit, and when she opened her life to Jesus, she opened her home to his followers. True faith is marked by changed behaviour. As James asks, 'What good is it... if someone claims to have faith but has no deeds?' (James 2:14). He is not saying that we can earn our place in God's family by our good deeds, but rather that genuine faith will be marked by godly behaviour. Lydia's hospitality was so warm that when Paul and Silas were released from prison, they went immediately to her home, sure of a welcome.

We're focusing on the women in Acts, but it is interesting to trace Luke's movements through the 'we' passages. In 16:7–8 we read, 'they came... they tried', but in verse 10–11, 'we got ready... we put out to sea.' In verse 40, 'they left'. The implication is that Luke joined Paul in Troas but stayed behind in Philippi to look after the infant church there.

Lord, may my home as well as my heart be open for you.

ROSEMARY GREEN

An unholy spirit

We met a slave-girl who had a spirit of divination and brought her owners a great deal of money by fortune-telling. While she followed Paul and us, she would cry out, 'These men are slaves of the Most High God, who proclaim to you a way of salvation.'

I have never questioned the reality and variety of the demons that Jesus encountered. Many of the people he met were not just physically or mentally ill; often the root cause of their disease was an evil spirit. For a long time, however, I thought, 'Surely not in this modern age.' Then I began to wonder whether perhaps in countries where evil spirits were actively worshipped, possession by evil spirits might be real—but still, surely not in the sophisticated West.

I was glad, in 1974, to read a book by an Englishwoman, Doreen Irvine, who wrote of her experience of being freed from evil spirits. That prepared me to meet, face to face, a woman who had had spiritual powers since childhood and had been deep in witchcraft. I had never before encountered evil in such stark form or recognised its power. My knees shook! Was Jesus really stronger?

Over the years, I learnt more of the power of Christ than I have learnt through anything else. I saw the woman released from demon after demon (sometimes in quite humorous situations). I saw her entrust herself to Jesus. I saw how strong, too, was the love of Jesus to woo souls. God gave me a particular gift of love for this very unlovely woman; ten years later, she told me how important that love (and the love of another couple) were in holding her through the many spiritual battles that ensued. Now I see a woman who loves Jesus and can hear him speaking to her more clearly than most Christians I know. We might call her a modern Mary Magdalene.

We do not need to look for demons under every bed, but we can be aware of their reality even in our world today.

I praise you, Lord, that your power and your love are stronger than all the forces of evil.

ROSEMARY GREEN

Marriage and ministry

Paul left Athens and went to Corinth. There he found a Jew named Aquila, a native of Pontus, who had recently come from Italy with his wife Priscilla... Paul went to see them, and because he was a tentmaker as they were, he stayed and worked with them.

One of the big advantages, for me, of being married to a clergyman is the privilege of being able to share his life in a way that is impossible in most professions. Of course, our roles and our gifts are different, but we love the togetherness when we can share in the same ministry.

Aquila and Priscilla were a remarkable couple. Aquila, originally from northern Turkey, was probably a freed slave in a well-to-do Roman home, who had married the daughter of the house (more shades of *Downton Abbey*). Their names are always mentioned together, but not always in the same order, which says a lot about their partnership. An imperial edict in AD49 expelled all Jews from Rome, so they emigrated to the cosmopolitan city of Corinth, where Paul met them the following year. Whether the three were initially drawn together by shared faith or shared trade is not clear. Paul came as a guest and stayed as a friend and fellow worker for 18 months—another example of the gift of hospitality.

As Priscilla and Aquila heard Paul preach, first in the synagogue and later in the home of Titus Justus, their faith took deeper root. We can imagine many conversations about Jesus and about the scriptures as they lived and worked together, and their shared joy as they saw many, both Jews and Gentiles, baptised.

It is lovely when we see Christian couples as close together in life and faith as Priscilla and Aquila were. I grieve for the 'limping couples' I know of, in which just one is a Christian; they cannot share the most important thing in life. I wish I could say that I pray regularly for each by name. Intermittently? Yes. Regularly? To my shame, no.

Make a list of 'limping couples' you know. Seek to pray for them regularly —for wisdom, graciousness and perseverance for the believer, and for a change of heart in the not-yet-Christian.

ROSEMARY GREEN

Flexibility

After staying [in Corinth] for a considerable time, Paul said farewell to the believers and sailed for Syria, accompanied by Priscilla and Aquila... When they reached Ephesus, he left them there.

Priscilla and Aquila had only been in Corinth for two or three years—just time to adapt to a new way of life, make friends and get established—but when Paul left to start his return journey to Antioch, they left too, travelling across the Aegean Sea to Ephesus. The Jews in the synagogue at Ephesus wanted to hear more from Paul, but, committed to his journey, he left the couple to continue his work. In their new home, we find them entertaining another guest, Apollos. They probably introduced him to the Holy Spirit, for 'he knew only the baptism of John' (v. 25). Their home was also a meeting-place for the Christians (1 Corinthians 16:19).

1 Corinthians was probably written in AD54, but when Paul wrote to the Romans a few years later, Priscilla and Aquila were back in Rome, after the emperor had died and the expulsion order on Jews had been lifted. Again, they hosted a church meeting in their house. Romans 16:3–5 gives another insight into their dedication: 'they risked their lives for me'—how or when, we don't know, but probably in the early days in Corinth, when Paul needed the encouragement of God's promise in Acts 18:9–10. By the time Paul wrote to Timothy in AD64, they were back in Ephesus again.

Perhaps they were just a restless couple who loved to travel and went where business was good, but I see people who were dedicated to the Lord and went where he called them to be useful for him. Moving house is not easy, and such mobility implied that they sat loose to possessions, that they were flexible and adaptable, not needing to cling to their circumstances or their way of life for security. A tree whose roots go deep can withstand the storm's buffeting.

Paul's phrase 'rooted and grounded in love' comes to mind. Read Ephesians 3:14–19, think about where your security lies, and pray that prayer for yourself.

ROSEMARY GREEN

A prophetic gift

We reached Caesarea and stayed at the house of Philip the
evangelist, one of the Seven. He had four unmarried daughters
who prophesied. After we had been there a number of days, a
prophet named Agabus came down from Judea.

Here were four sisters whose father was a red-hot evangelist (see Acts
8:4–8, 26–40). Sometimes such people win others for Christ but
neglect their own families, and their offspring rebel. Not so with Philip,
whom we find returning home after meeting the Ethiopian eunuch.

We do not know how Philip's daughters developed or used their prophetic gifts; I guess they helped one another. But what do we mean by
'prophecy'? I define it as 'a message given directly by God to enlighten
others'. Years ago, our son commented, 'Prophecy is not a *new* message but a *now* message.' Prophecy in our day will neither add to scripture nor contradict it, although it may underline it. It may come as
an encouragement (Acts 18:9–10) or a warning, like Agabus' prophecy
here and in 11:28–30.

I remember two occasions in our former church. Near the end of the
service, a student tentatively approached the minister, saying, 'I think I
have a message from God for the congregation.' The minister showed
the written message to the visiting archbishop; both thought that part
of it was from God, and part just from the young man. The first section
was read aloud and rang true with us all.

The other situation was a personal one. My husband was wrestling
over a possible job overseas: his head said 'yes' and heart said 'no'.
With no upfront part in one evening service, he sat in a pew beside a
stranger. Before the service closed, the verger spoke up from the back.
Luke 9:62 had a personalised twist: 'No one who puts a hand to the
plough and looks back is fit for service in the kingdom of God.' Wham!
The stranger turned and said, 'Excuse me. I know nothing of your situation, but I believe that word was for you.' Wham again! This was a
prophetic word given in public for an individual.

---

*Lord, please help me to be sensitive and obedient to your voice, and
willing to risk passing it on to others.*

ROSEMARY GREEN

The silent consorts

Several days later Felix came with his wife Drusilla, who was Jewish. He sent for Paul and listened to him as he spoke about faith in Jesus... Agrippa and Bernice came with great pomp and entered the audience room... At the command of Festus, Paul was brought in.

Aquila and Priscilla, Felix and Drusilla had one thing in common: both couples were mixed marriages between a Roman and a Jew, but there the similarity ends. In status, in character and in faith, they were opposites. Felix, 'who was well acquainted with the Way' (Acts 24:22), listened many times to Paul's defence of his faith, but primarily because he hoped for a bribe. Whether Drusilla was with him at these times, we don't know. She was his third wife and was still only a teenager when he married her, having persuaded her to leave her first (arranged) marriage to a petty Syrian king. Perhaps Drusilla hoped that this would mean advancement in her status. Such behaviour was typical of a member of the Herod family, a dynasty in which unfaithfulness, divorce, murder, incest and remarriage were the norm.

Bernice and Drusilla were sisters, the oldest and youngest offspring of Herod Agrippa (the Herod who killed James and arrested Peter, as we read in Acts 12). Bernice's marital life was even more colourful than Drusilla's. Aged 13, she married her uncle Herod of Chalci. Seven years later, he died and she began an incestuous relationship with her brother, Herod Agrippa II. She married Polemon, king of Cilicia, but then deserted him and returned to her brother, with whom she heard Paul speak. She later became the mistress of the Roman general Titus and the emperor Vespasian. What a sad muddle!

It is easy to condemn such behaviour as totally unacceptable (which it is), but Jesus warned us to take the plank out of our own eye before trying to remove the splinter from another's (Matthew 7:5). Paul wrote similarly in Romans 2:1. Beware of smug criticism!

Don't be afraid to ask God to show you any impurity in your own relationships. Then ask him to assure you of his forgiveness and cleansing.

ROSEMARY GREEN

Making links

Margaret Killingray writes:

We are going to be looking at the lives of two Old Testament characters who lived nearly 3000 years ago—Hezekiah and Daniel. Old Testament history can sometimes seem a little dull and not particularly relevant to our lives today. Yet when we look closely at the men and women who appear in its pages, we see that, despite the differences of time, culture and geography, their ups and downs, their struggles and their failures are not so different from ours. They faced problems within their families and with their public duties. They lived in times of famine and war, plenty and peace. Some of them turned away from the Lord, forgetting his commands and serving pagan gods.

Hezekiah was a king of Judah, and Daniel was an adviser to the kings of Babylon. Both found themselves with heavy responsibilities in very difficult situations, but they trusted God and used their skills and intelligence to serve him and his people. Hezekiah's story is told in three books: 2 Kings, 2 Chronicles and the book of Isaiah, the prophet who helped and advised him. When Hezekiah was king, Israel was two separate states. 200 years before him, after the reign of Solomon, it had split in two, with Israel (Samaria) to the north and Judah, with Jerusalem the capital, to the south. Six years into his 29-year reign, Samaria was conquered by the Assyrians and many of its people were taken into exile. The same fate overtook Judah around 70 years after Hezekiah's death, when Daniel and many of his fellow Jews were taken into exile to serve the kings of Babylon.

Seek first the kingdom of God

Hezekiah trusted in the Lord, the God of Israel. There was no one like him among all the kings of Judah, either before or after him. He held fast to the Lord and did not stop following him; he kept the commands the Lord had given Moses.

Hezekiah's father had not held fast to the Lord: he worshipped many other gods, including sacrificing some of his children to one god by throwing them into the altar fire. So, when he became king, Hezekiah was determined to follow the commands of the Lord and to serve his people well. He began by clearing out all the altars to foreign gods and opening up the temple, which had been shut up and abandoned by his father. He reinstated the priests and musicians and ordered them to begin regular times of worship and praise, once again, singing the psalms of David with joy and gladness.

It would never be easy, though; Hezekiah reigned over a small area round Jerusalem, always threatened by other powers—Assyria, Babylon and Egypt. After Samaria was conquered, enemies were never far away.

What can we learn from Hezekiah's example? Like him, wherever we have responsibilities today, within our families and churches, running a business or just one desk, or even running a country, we too are called to seek God's kingdom first. That may not always be straightforward. We too live in a messy and sometimes hostile world. It's hard to teach science in a school where most of the staff are sceptical non-believers. It's hard to have a responsible job in a company where some fellow directors are pushing the boundaries of legality. It's hard to be a parent and watch a child abandon faith and the church and take up a very different lifestyle.

Hezekiah probably realised that his own son would be a bad king. The good we have done may be swept away by those coming after us, but the promise is that all we have done to build the Lord's kingdom will count in the end, when he comes again.

Do you know someone who is having a hard time? Maybe they need you to listen to them and pray with them, helping them to see the wider picture.

MARGARET KILLINGRAY

A wonderful celebration

The Israelites who were present in Jerusalem celebrated the Festival of Unleavened Bread for seven days with great rejoicing, while the Levites and priests praised the Lord every day with resounding instruments to the Lord... The whole assembly then agreed to celebrate the festival seven more days.

It's great to sing songs of praise at special times, whether it is carols at Christmas or resurrection Easter hymns. Hezekiah decided to celebrate Passover (the festival that recalled Israel's rescue from slavery in Egypt) in the newly restored temple in Jerusalem. He invited everyone in Judah and he also sent invitations to the people in the conquered northern kingdom, Samaria, now ruled by Assyria. Many who came were not sure what was going on and hadn't prepared and purified themselves according to the regulations laid down by Moses. There were non-Jews, aliens from the north, perhaps even one or two Assyrians—but there were no exclusions and Hezekiah simply prayed that the Lord would accept the honest worship, however hazy, of all of them. There was a lot of feasting, singing, music and praise.

Maybe, in our churches and home groups, we should sometimes bend the rules a bit—consciously relax our style, just have a meal and some chatting, use different kinds of music and alternative worship styles. In the UK, well over 90 per cent of adults hardly ever go to church, and many of them cannot understand how relatively sane people can actually belong to a church and be followers of Jesus Christ. We may need to find ways to throw open the doors to the suspicious and the critical—Christmas parties for the local children; an arts group, quiz nights with wine—and let them wonder what it's all about, not telling them the full story until they *really* want to know. Perhaps we could accept the odd 'Assyrian' and simply pray in our hearts that those who seek—over a nice meal and a bit of a chat—will find, in the end, the Lord of the Passover, who still invites all who hunger and thirst to join him.

Read Exodus 12:1–14, where the origin of the Passover is described. Is there an excuse for a celebration in your fellowship?

MARGARET KILLINGRAY

We all make mistakes!

Sennacherib king of Assyria attacked the fortified cities of Judah and captured them. So Hezekiah king of Judah sent this message… 'I have done wrong. Withdraw from me, and I will pay whatever you demand of me.' … Hezekiah gave him all the silver that was found in the temple of the Lord and in the treasuries of the royal palace.

Jerusalem was close to destruction. Sennacherib and his armies had already conquered Samaria and other nations not far from Judah. Hezekiah and his people knew that they might lose everything and end up dead or slaves, so Hezekiah tried to buy off Sennacherib with all the treasures he had used to repair the temple. It didn't work: Sennacherib took the treasure and continued to attack.

Was Hezekiah wrong to be apologetic and try to buy off his cruel enemy? I expect he was desperate enough to try anything. He also did practical things in defence of Jerusalem, such as reinforcing the walls and blocking off the springs outside the city to deprive the attackers of water. Mistakes are not always sin; they are often the outcome of a limited knowledge of circumstances. Sometimes we have to jump in and, like Hezekiah, do the best we can, trusting God for the outcome. We are often quick to blame each other and our leaders for mistakes that are part of being human and not knowing everything.

In the end, it made no difference. Sennacherib's campaign against Judah was now freshly funded—by his victim. Hezekiah had to trust God alone to save them. Dealing with mistakes honestly, putting them right and admitting we were wrong are some of the hardest things we have to do, particularly if others depend on our leadership, but that can be the beginning of a refreshed relationship with the Lord and other people.

When someone makes a mistake that affects us, we need to reassure rather than demand recompense and repentance, and tell them that we understand. Christian disciples are not the 'always good' but the 'often forgiven'. They obey God out of love and gratitude and they sometimes make mistakes. (Sennacherib never did conquer Jerusalem.)

Sometimes trivial mistakes bother us far more than they should. If we can't put it right, we need to pray about it and leave it with the Lord.

MARGARET KILLINGRAY

A war of words

[Sennacherib sent this message] 'When Hezekiah says, "The Lord our God will save us from the hand of the king of Assyria," he is misleading you, to let you die of hunger and thirst... Were the gods of [other] nations ever able to deliver their land from my hand?'

In the British Museum there are stone panels from Sennacherib's palace in Nineveh, which show the capture of Lachish, a town near Jerusalem: the inhabitants trudge into captivity far from home and its officials are tortured and executed. The Assyrians assumed that, given half a chance, Jerusalem would surrender rather than face a long siege, so Sennacherib sent his field commander with a large army to Jerusalem and, under the walls of the city, the commander delivered his message for Hezekiah loudly so that all the people standing on the walls would hear.

The message questioned their faith in God and questioned Hezekiah's confidence that God would act to save Judah, since most of Judah's towns had already been captured. It made fun of Judah's military strength: 'I will give you 2000 horses, if you could put riders on them!' (Isaiah 36:8). According to Isaiah, Sennacherib's final blasphemous insult was, 'Furthermore, have I come to attack and destroy this land without the Lord? The Lord himself told me to march against this country and destroy it' (v. 10).

Many of us know this kind of attack; sometimes, from within us, a voice tells us that we can't possibly achieve a particular task or that we are no good at our job. Sometimes a family member keeps telling us how to bring up our children or how to make our cooking more interesting. I know of children who have been undermined by sarcastic teachers. It is very difficult to face the voices telling us that God simply doesn't answer prayers or that miracles only happened in the past. We all need the loving support and prayerful care of friends when we face undermining doubt that begins to destroy our faith and our confidence in the Lord.

It is hard to admit we are having doubts and finding prayer difficult. Again we need to turn to a friend we trust, and talk things through and pray together.

MARGARET KILLINGRAY

When it's all too much!

Hezekiah received the letter from the messengers and read it. Then he went up to the temple of the Lord and spread it out before the Lord. And Hezekiah prayed to the Lord: '… Give ear, Lord, and hear; open your eyes, Lord, and see; listen to the words Sennacherib has sent to ridicule the living God.'

Poor Hezekiah! First, Sennacherib's field commander shouted his challenge at Jerusalem, insulting the Lord, then Isaiah told him not to be afraid, then Sennacherib sent a letter telling him that no god could protect Jerusalem from his attack. So he went to the temple of the Lord, taking the letter with him. He spread it out and told God to read it! But, of course, God knew all about it even before it happened. It wasn't God who was fearful, who didn't know what to do; it was Hezekiah, and he ended his desperate prayer, 'Now, Lord our God, deliver us… so that all the kingdoms of the earth may know that you alone, Lord, are God' (v. 19). Then there were footsteps behind him; a messenger from Isaiah told him that God had heard his prayer and his answer was that Sennacherib would not enter the city. God would defend the city and save it.

In the last three verses of this chapter, we find out how Jerusalem was saved. The writer tells us that the angel of the Lord passed over the Assyrian army and a very large number of the soldiers died that night. Maybe they had drunk polluted water, since Hezekiah had blocked up the water sources. We don't know how they died, but we do know that Sennacherib went back to Nineveh, where two of his sons murdered him.

God does answer prayer. Many people I know have experienced answers—though not always exactly what they prayed for, and not always straight away. When we are presented with a desperate problem—a bill we can't pay or a loved one's serious illness, for example—we could show God the bill, the letter or the photograph, and simply lay the problem before him. Sometimes that is all we can do.

How do you plan your prayer times? Read James 5:13–18, about prayer, and, if you have time, 2 Corinthians 12:7b–10, where Paul's prayer was not answered as he had hoped.

MARGARET KILLINGRAY

I believe in the resurrection

[Hezekiah] said, 'In the prime of my life must I go through the gates of death and be robbed of the rest of my years? ... For the grave cannot praise you, death cannot sing your praise; those who go down to the pit cannot hope for your faithfulness. The living, the living—they praise you.'

Hezekiah was ill and Isaiah told him he would die. The storyteller says that Hezekiah turned his face to the wall, prayed and wept bitterly. Then he voiced one of the great cries of the human heart. 'Is death the end? Is all that I have done going to fade and go to waste? I am not ready to die; I have so many things to do.'

It seems that, in Old Testament times, there was only a very hazy idea about a life after death. Jesus said to Martha, before he brought her brother Lazarus back from the dead, 'I am the resurrection and the life. The one who believes in me will live, even though they die' (John 11:25). Hezekiah did not have that certainty, but when he did reach heaven as a faithful servant of the living God, how great must have been his joy and surprise to join in the praises of his Saviour, a man like himself!

The Lord answered Hezekiah's despairing prayer, sending Isaiah to treat his symptoms and to promise him 15 more years of peace and protection. This illness happened before Sennacherib's attack, so when the attack failed and the Assyrian armies went away, Hezekiah knew he had time—time to govern well, with more opportunities to put things right. Being 'born again' as Christians, in a way, means that we have another go at life. Much may need forgiving; consequences of past sins need sorting out, but we can start again. Each fresh day of our life, the Lord says to us, 'Get up and go! Love your neighbour; forgive those who sin against you; build the kingdom at work, at home and wherever you are.' Then one day we too will be raised from death and will see him face to face.

Read the story of Jesus and Lazarus in John 11. How Lazarus must have rejoiced when Jesus rose from the dead! Pray for fresh assurance of the truth of the resurrection.

MARGARET KILLINGRAY

Living as exiles

By the rivers of Babylon we sat and wept when we remembered Zion. There on the poplars we hung our harps, for there our captors asked us for songs… They said, 'Sing us one of the songs of Zion!' How can we sing the songs of the Lord while in a foreign land?

Jerusalem was peaceful for a whole generation after Hezekiah's death. Then another king, Nebuchadnezzar from Babylon, conquered the city. Thousands of Israelites were taken into exile; many became slaves, cheap labour in the fields and cities of Babylon. Psalm 137 is a cry of despair and longing for their distant homeland.

However, the king ordered that some of the young men should serve him in his palace. Daniel and three of his friends—all fit, handsome and clever—were chosen (Daniel 1:4). As prisoners of war, having seen their city and its temple destroyed and been forced to march through miles of desert, they had lost family, culture, language and all the customs and comforts of home. How could they 'sing the songs of the Lord' surrounded by the false gods and idols, the magicians and astrologers, in the palace of the king of Babylon?

Forced exile is very hard to endure. Today millions of refugees are exiled, displaced from familiar homes and cities by war and hunger. As I write, the news is full of terrible stories from Syria of families fleeing their homes to live in vast refugee camps. Some have fled to Iraq, where the ruins of Babylon stand near the great River Euphrates. They need our prayers and our support for the many relief agencies helping them. Yet 'exile' is one of the biblical pictures of our lives on earth. Peter calls us 'aliens and strangers' in the world, while the letter to the Hebrews tells us we have no enduring city, but are looking for the city that is to come (13:14).

Rescued from 'slavery', we are led on a journey, always in temporary accommodation, onwards to a perfect home, and until we get there we are never totally at home. In another sense, however, if we belong to Jesus, wherever we are, we are at home with him.

Are there new people at church or in your street? Are there people living on their own with families far away? Can we help them feel at home?
                                                                    MARGARET KILLINGRAY

Engaging with the world

The king talked with them, and he found none equal to Daniel, Hananiah, Mishael and Azariah; so they entered the king's service. In every matter of wisdom and understanding about which the king questioned them, he found them ten times better than all the magicians and enchanters in his whole kingdom.

On the king's orders, Daniel and his three companions spent three years learning the language and literature of the Babylonians, during which time Daniel developed the ability to interpret dreams and visions. They were still prisoners: they could have refused to cooperate and would probably have ended up enslaved or dead; they could have simply given up hope and faith in God and done what they were told. Instead, though, Daniel and his friends went to the enemy's schools, learnt the language, read the literature and engaged with this alien pagan culture. They did take one step to maintain their independence as servants of the one true God: they refused to eat the rich food and wine allocated to them from the king's kitchens. They chose to eat only vegetables and drink only water. They established their difference, as believers in the God of Israel, with humility and self-discipline. They responded to their guards and captors with courtesy and consideration.

As Christians in a secular, sometimes anti-Christian culture, how do we relate to the world around us? What do we watch on television? How do we spend our leisure time? How do we relate to colleagues and neighbours? Someone once said that Christians in the world are sometimes chameleons, fading into the colour of the culture, doing what everyone else does. Sometimes they are ostriches with heads in the sand, avoiding, as far as possible, all contact with the non-Christian world. Sometimes they are porcupines with hackles up, harshly confronting and criticising everyone and everything they disapprove of. Daniel chose to understand the world he was in, to show love and courtesy to all, but also to let them know he was a servant of the living God.

Read 2 Corinthians 5:16–21, where Paul tells his readers that God has committed to them the message of reconciliation as Christ's ambassadors. Being ambassadors and reconcilers requires love and tact.

MARGARET KILLINGRAY

But if not

'King Nebuchadnezzar... if we are thrown into the blazing furnace, the God we serve is able to deliver us from it... But even if he does not, we want you to know, Your Majesty, that we will not serve your gods or worship the image of gold you have set up.'

The king gave top jobs to Daniel and his three companions, who were now given Babylonian names—Shadrach, Meshach and Abednego. Then he decided that his civil servants and governors needed a lesson in obedience. He made a golden idol and ordered them all to bow down to it. If they refused, they would die in a blazing furnace.

For Daniel's three friends, the story had a miraculous ending as they walked out of the fire unharmed. Nebuchadnezzar and his officials were overwhelmed with amazement, especially as they had seen a god-like figure walking with the three in the fire. But Shadrach and his companions did not know what the outcome would be when they refused to obey the king. Disciples of the Lord have no guarantee of special favours. There are Christians today who face persecution for their faith, who have to say, 'Our God can save us, but if he does not, we will not deny him to save ourselves.'

There is a story that an army officer organising the evacuation of troops from the beaches of Dunkirk in 1940 sent his family a telegram that simply said, 'But if not...' He knew they would know what he meant. He longed for rescue but he would trust God, whatever the outcome. Most of us do not have to face such challenging situations. When we long with all our hearts for an outcome that matters very much—our healing from a life-threatening illness, an end to being bullied at work or the conception of a longed-for child—we too have to say, 'But if not...', knowing that our Lord walks with us in the fiery places. We know, too, that 'in all things God works for the good of those who love him, who have been called according to his purpose' (Romans 8:28).

When facing up to 'But if not...' situations, we can become angry or full of doubt. Then we should remember Jesus in Gethsemane and on the cross—and the darkness that ended in resurrection light.

MARGARET KILLINGRAY

Kings are humbled

Now I, Nebuchadnezzar, praise and exalt and glorify the King of heaven, because everything he does is right and all his ways are just. And those who walk in pride he is able to humble.

Daniel had the God-given gift of being able to interpret dreams. Early in his time at Nebuchadnezzar's court, the king had been troubled by dreams. He demanded that his court magicians tell him what the dreams meant—but he also refused to tell them what exactly he had dreamt! When they couldn't answer him, he gave orders that all the wise men, including Daniel, should be executed. God revealed the meaning of the dream to Daniel, who immediately went to the king to save the magicians and wise men. Nebuchadnezzar bowed down to Daniel, saying, 'Surely your God is the God of gods and the Lord of kings' (Daniel 2:47).

The king soon forgot Daniel's God, however, and went back to the old idols. Near the end of his reign, he had another dream that told him he would become mad and be driven out of his city to live among the wild animals—and so it happened. 'His body was drenched with the dew of heaven until his hair grew like the feathers of an eagle and his nails like the claws of a bird' (4:33). Finally his sanity was restored and his last recorded words were praise of the one true God, the King of heaven.

Daniel, who may have retired when the king died, was summoned once more when the next king, Belshazzar, held a great feast of drunken splendour. Belshazzar sent for all the gold and silver goblets that had been stolen from the temple in Jerusalem, for the use of 'his nobles, his wives and concubines' (5:3). Then suddenly a moving finger wrote on the wall, and eventually Daniel was called to face this drunk and rather scared bully and tell him what the writing said. Again Daniel told the truth: this king had learnt nothing and judgement was about to fall. The next day, Darius the Persian was in charge and Belshazzar was dead.

Some people have to work for petty tyrants and unpredictable bosses. Sometimes we have to speak the truth as Daniel did. In our small groups, do we pray for such difficult situations?

MARGARET KILLINGRAY

Daniel, jealousy and some lions

The king planned to set [Daniel] over the whole kingdom. At this, the chief ministers... tried to find grounds for charges against Daniel in his conduct of government affairs, but they were unable to do so... Finally these men said, 'We will never find any basis for charges against this man Daniel unless it has something to do with the law of his God.'

Darius the Persian faced many challenges in ruling a conquered people and he came to rely on Daniel's trustworthiness, but Daniel was a foreign exile and many of the other officials were jealous of his promotion. The only way they could catch him out was to challenge his faith in his God, so they proposed a period of religious observance during which Darius alone, as 'divine' king, would receive the people's prayers. Darius was very flattered and signed the decree. Anyone who refused would be thrown into the lions' den.

Daniel continued to pray regularly to the living God with his windows open towards Jerusalem. Perhaps Darius, new to Babylon, didn't know anything about the God whom Daniel worshipped, and he was deeply distressed when he discovered that he had signed Daniel's death warrant, with no way of backing down. Darius himself sealed the rock over the lion's cave entrance, with Daniel inside, and then spent a sleepless night, hurrying at dawn to see if Daniel was still alive. Daniel emerged unscathed, saying, 'My God sent his angel, and he shut the mouths of the lions... Nor have I ever done any wrong before you, Your Majesty' (v. 22). Darius issued a decree that, in all parts of his kingdom, people must fear and reverence the God of Daniel. Once again, Daniel's integrity, faithfulness and courtesy had won a powerful convert.

The challenge for us, living in a world where many do not honour or even believe in our Lord and Saviour, is to maintain a witness of love and commitment at work and in our communities, where sometimes we will meet a challenge to our Christian principles that means we will have to take a stand. (Fortunately there will be no problem with lions!)

Read Galatians 5:13–26, where Paul helps Christians to understand what it means to live by the Spirit, loving their neighbours and avoiding the temptations around them.

MARGARET KILLINGRAY

Daniel prays for his people

I, Daniel, understood from the Scriptures, according to the word of the Lord given to Jeremiah the prophet, that the desolation of Jerusalem would last seventy years... I prayed to the Lord my God and confessed: '... Now, our God, hear the prayers and petitions of your servant... For your sake, my God, do not delay.'

We are told that Daniel prayed regularly—three times a day, with his window open. People walking by could see him at prayer. He may have covered all the usual topics—friends with problems, wisdom for his work, and so on. I'm sure he prayed for his fellow Jews who worked long hours as slaves. We know he had some of the Hebrew scriptures and may have used the psalms as prayers.

One day, he read in the book of Jeremiah that the exile would last for 70 years. It seems likely that Daniel was already well on in years, so he knew he would never see Jerusalem again, but he realised that God had allowed the conquest of Judah and the people's exile because of their unfaithfulness. Such a terrible disaster had to be an indication that their sin and disobedience had been very great. Would the Lord simply let them go back after 70 years, whatever their attitude to him? Daniel knew there had to be a recognition of their sin and an act of repentance, so he began a passionate prayer of repentance and shame, identifying himself with his people: 'We have sinned and done wrong; we have been wicked and have rebelled; we have turned away from your commands and laws' (v. 5).

Daniel was in a privileged position—honoured by the kings of Babylon, given responsibility for running the country, well fed and well housed—but he took it upon himself to pray for all his people, to share their shame and to throw himself on the mercy of God. In a way he reminds me of Jesus himself, the sinless Son of God, who bore in his body the sins of the whole world so that we could find full forgiveness and one day be with him for ever in the new Jerusalem.

Lord, when someone we know, even someone we love, disregards your laws and acts in hurtful and destructive ways, help us pray for them with Daniel's passion.

MARGARET KILLINGRAY

Daniel's visions

While I, Daniel, was watching the vision and trying to understand
it, there before me stood one who looked like a man... As he
came near the place where I was standing, I was terrified and fell
prostrate. 'Son of man,' he said to me, 'understand that the vision
concerns the time of the end.'

Daniel experienced dreams and visions; other Old Testament prophets
also had visions, as did John, recording them in the book of Revelation.
Sometimes there is an explanation, but not always. Practical, down-to-
earth 21st-century people don't find it easy to understand the role of
visions and dreams that foretell the future.

Daniel must have wondered whether all God's plans had fizzled out
in the ruins of Jerusalem, with his people scattered. Would Jeremiah's
prophetic vision ever become real? Would the city he longed for ever be
rebuilt? God spoke in visions that said, in effect, 'Don't imagine that these
tawdry kingdoms, ruled by petty tyrants, are anything more than a blip
in time. The times are in my hands and always have been. The end will
come as I have always planned. Be assured that I am the reality and the
truth behind the created universe and the whole history of this world.'

Daniel never saw Jerusalem again but he recorded the visions which
convinced him that the glory of Jerusalem would be restored. The city
was rebuilt some time later, and the exiles were allowed to travel back
to their homes, with the blessing of a later king of Babylon. Yet once
more, 40 years after Jesus' resurrection, Jerusalem and its temple were
destroyed, this time by the Romans. Today, those who worship Hezekiah's and Daniel's God come from every nation on earth and they look
for the heavenly city, the new Jerusalem where one day we will all gather.

We should take these biblical visions seriously and accept that we
may not realise their full meaning until they are completely fulfilled,
when Jesus comes again. Meanwhile, like Daniel, we are called to work
to encourage human flourishing, engaging with our culture and looking
forward to the greater reality that we call heaven.

---

*Some people find it hard to get to grips with Old Testament history. Some
need help to pull out an exciting story yet retain the text's important
points. Can you do that?*

MARGARET KILLINGRAY

The God of history

Listen! Your watchmen lift up their voices; together they shout for joy. When the Lord returns to Zion, they will see it with their own eyes. Burst into songs of joy together, you ruins of Jerusalem, for the Lord has comforted his people, he has redeemed Jerusalem.

We have read the stories of two men—a king and a servant of kings; both sought to serve the Lord their God in difficult times. We, who live in a messy world thousands of years later, can seek to learn from the way they handled their problems, but that is not what these stories are about. Underlying them is a far greater story, a far bigger and more important truth. They are only very small moments in the whole history of God's purposes and plans, from creation to his final redemption and re-creation of all things.

Jeremiah and Isaiah were prophets who understood that the conquest and destruction of Jerusalem were a consequence of the people's disobedience and betrayal of all that God had taught them through Moses and their other leaders and prophets. They knew enough of God's character to know that he would forgive and restore them to their homeland, the temple would be rebuilt and Jerusalem would rise from the ashes. But Isaiah also saw that the Lord would send a redeemer and saviour, who would be 'a man of suffering, and familiar with pain... He was pierced for our transgressions, he was crushed for our iniquities; the punishment that brought us peace was on him' (Isaiah 53:3, 5).

There were joy and delight and songs of praise when Hezekiah restored the temple; there was celebration when the exiles returned to Jerusalem and rebuilt the walls and the temple; and one day there will be a joyful celebration and reunion of all God's people in a new heaven and a new earth. As John describes that day, in Revelation 21:2–4, 'I saw the Holy City, the new Jerusalem… God's dwelling-place is now among the people... He will wipe every tear from their eyes.'

'Therefore go and make disciples... teaching them to obey everything I have commanded you. And surely I am with you always, to the end of the age' (Matthew 28:19–20). That is our part in the history of the world.
MARGARET KILLINGRAY

Making links

Christine Platt writes:

Deep within our hearts we yearn for a world characterised by goodness, truth and justice, where every man, woman and child is treated with dignity and everyone's needs for food, clothing, shelter, medical care and basic human rights are met. No wonder our hearts plummet to our boots when we read newspapers or watch TV news: instead, there is mayhem and madness.

A recent news item that appalled me was about the manufacture and sale of 'legal highs'. Some people are so driven by greed that their hearts are closed to human misery. Others justify selling these drugs by saying, 'I've got to make a living too', even when faced with distraught mothers whose teenagers are being destroyed by them. In a just society, this could not happen. On the world scene, two-thirds of the six billion of us live precariously on less than $2 per day, while one-third enjoys a much higher standard of living and security. This is not fair.

When God looked, he 'was displeased that there was no justice… he was appalled that there was no one to intervene' (Isaiah 59:15–16). Throughout the ages, he sent people to remind us of our true destiny, a fair and just world, and our responsibilities to work towards it. He gave clear instructions to Moses about how to treat the vulnerable—aliens, poor, fatherless and widows. He sent judges to exercise honest leadership and prophets to hammer his message home.

There have been startling breakthroughs, where people have fought tenaciously to break entrenched unjust attitudes and laws and justice has blossomed like a rose. Some examples are the abolition of the slave trade, the dismantling of apartheid in South Africa and equal rights for black and white in the USA. Sadly, new injustices lurch into view as soon as one is defeated. This reveals the poisonous, twisted mind of our enemy, who relishes the sight of defenceless people being exploited.

Over these two weeks we will look at God's heart of compassion and mercy and his passionate longing for justice. We will also see how his people have turned the tide of evil and established justice. We will learn from their examples about how we can work for justice in our own location and bring joy to God's heart as well as our fellow human beings.

Does God care?

Into the hovels of the poor, into the dark streets where the
homeless groan, God speaks: 'I've had enough; I'm on my way to
heal the ache in the heart of the wretched.'

In this psalm David beseeches God for help. Life is just too hard. People lie and deceive; evil is rampant. David is almost in despair.

There have been many times throughout humanity's dark history when no spark of godliness has seemed apparent. We've even descended to the state where 'what is vile is honoured by the human race' (v. 8, NIV). People have lost sight of what is noble and good. Instead they (we) worship at the cathedrals of consumerism (the shopping centres), squander resources at casinos instead of caring for children, and laugh at smutty jokes; loan sharks prey on the financially naïve... the list goes on.

Is God sitting up in heaven wringing his hands in impotence or has he simply turned away in disgust? This psalm emphatically declares that God sees and God cares. He sees the substandard housing where infections run riot. He knows every homeless person huddled under a bridge. He hears every groan, whatever its cause, and he is 'on [his] way to heal the ache in the heart of the wretched'.

This psalm goes on to proclaim the purity of God's word, and that this word has been tested and found to be trustworthy and true.

For us to live rightly and be instruments of his truth in this world, we need to have our minds informed and transformed so that we are not deceived into accepting this world's standards, where 'what is vile is honoured'. God's word will keep us on track so that we are not led away by the lies of the enemy. He is 'a liar and the father of lies' (John 8:44, NIV). He is clearly spreading his poison very effectively. We need to be vigilant and resist, using the weapons God has given us (Ephesians 6:10–18).

Lord God, give me wisdom and courage to live according to your word.
Help me to work with you to 'heal the ache in the heart of the wretched'.
                                                                CHRISTINE PLATT

Enough is enough!

The Lord said, 'I have indeed seen the misery of my people in Egypt. I have heard them crying out because of their slave drivers, and I am concerned about their suffering. So I have come down to rescue them.'

God's chosen people, descendants of Abraham, were suffering cruel exploitation in Egypt. God saw their misery, he heard their cries, he was concerned, and he came down to rescue. His chosen agent on this occasion was an initially reluctant Moses who, unknowingly, had been on God's training programme for this task since his birth.

God planned to rescue his people and was going to send not a legion of powerful angels but just one elderly man, and, because of that man's fearful heart, his brother also. God promised to be with Moses and Aaron and to stretch out his mighty hand (vv. 19–20). The success of the mission was not in doubt in God's mind, although Moses wasn't quite so sure. As many of us do, Moses looked at his own limitations rather than at God's power and promises.

It was not easy. There were setbacks and much opposition. By Exodus 5:22–23, Moses is ready to give up and go home, complaining to God that things are worse instead of better: 'You have not rescued your people at all.' In response, God reaffirmed his promises and plans (Exodus 6). An awe-inspiring series of miracles then took place, during which time Moses grew in faith and confidence until he was ready to lead the people out of slavery: 'all the Lord's divisions left Egypt... the Lord kept vigil' (12:41–42). God delivered his people from injustice and gave them the opportunity to create a just society. He used an ordinary person as his agent.

God can use us in the same way to work for justice in our own locality. There will be opposition but, if we cooperate with God's programme, he will enable us to grow in faith, just as he did with Moses. His mighty hand is still at work.

Lord, open my eyes to the injustices around me and help me to know how I can be your agent to bring freedom to those who suffer.

CHRISTINE PLATT

God's plan for the poor

Boaz said to Ruth, 'My daughter, listen to me. Don't go and glean in another field and don't go away from here... I have told the men not to lay a hand on you. And whenever you are thirsty, go and get a drink from the water jars the men have filled.'

When God had rescued his people from oppression in Egypt, he gave them laws so that they could operate a just and caring society. One of these laws said, 'When you reap the harvest of your land, do not reap to the very edges of your field... Leave them for the poor and the foreigner' (Leviticus 19:9–10).

God knew that some people would have good business minds and rise up the financial ladder, whereas others would struggle. He wanted the vulnerable to be provided for. These farmers did not have to pick the grain and make bread to give to the poor. They needed to allow people to come on to their land and pick grain for themselves. Doing honest work gave people dignity and prevented dependency.

Boaz recognised that God had blessed him. He took God's commands seriously in his role as an employer and wealthy man. With Ruth he went the extra mile to make sure she was protected and cared for while she worked in his fields.

How can we apply this principle today? We could support organisations that strive to help people get into paid work, or organisations like Christians Against Poverty, which helps people to use their money wisely and get out of debt. The 'edges of our field' might include buying extra groceries to give to a food bank that also offers budgeting advice. If you know someone who is out of work, you could support them emotionally and in prayer: unemployment can be a very lonely experience. Encouraging them to volunteer in some capacity can help to keep them in a mindset of working while they pursue employment.

What one thing can you do this week to care for the poor in your area? Make it a weekly habit.

CHRISTINE PLATT

Seek the Lord and live

You trample on the poor and force him to give you grain... But let justice roll on like a river, righteousness like a never-failing stream!

Clearly Israel had not created the fair and just society that God had envisaged, so he sent Amos with a chilling message. Amos first calls to Israel to turn back to God, 'Seek the Lord and live' (v. 6), then to 'hate evil, love good' (v. 15). Their litany of sins was extensive:

- They had 'turned justice into bitterness' (v. 7). Something that was meant to be a way of ensuring justice was turned upside-down: the courts were corrupt.
- Those who told the truth were despised—possibly whistle-blowers (v. 10).
- The rich stole from the poor (v. 11): in our context, rich nations pay low prices for raw materials from developing nations and then make fat profits for themselves.

Even worse, they carried on their religious services as though all was well. God was not impressed. In fact, he hated and despised their hypocrisy and would not listen to them (vv. 21–23). God was looking for justice and right living. If the people didn't repent and mend their ways, he was going to send them into exile, away from their promised land (v. 27)—and this exile eventually took place.

We can sometimes feel impotent in the face of major injustice, such as persecution of Christians in other lands or the way the world economic system is so grossly unfair to developing nations. But, in Edward Burke's challenging statement, 'All that is necessary for evil to triumph is for good men [and women] to do nothing'. We need to do something, however small it might seem in our eyes: lots of small efforts combined can promote significant change. We can pray, sign petitions, and use our buying power wisely.

What particular area of injustice concerns you? Think of ways you can combine with others to stem the tide of evil.

CHRISTINE PLATT

Preparing to make a difference

When I heard these things, I sat down and wept. For some days I mourned and fasted and prayed before the God of heaven.

Nehemiah was part of the exiled Jewish people living in the Persian empire. He heard about a major problem in Jerusalem: the city walls were broken down so the inhabitants were defenceless against their enemies. Nehemiah took time to allow the awfulness of the situation to penetrate his heart: he mourned, fasted and prayed.

Sometimes it seems that our news is about one ghastly event after another—war, terrorism, domestic violence, hunger and sick children. We can't emotionally take on board all the world's pain, but, because there is so much of it, we can be tempted to let it glide over us with maybe a brief prayer and a consoling cup of tea.

The broken city wall was one issue that Nehemiah couldn't allow to glide over him, so he 'sat with it' for some days and a plan began to formulate in his mind. He took the opportunity presented to him and got permission from the king to go there. He had also thought carefully about the need for letters to guarantee him safe travel. On arrival in Jerusalem, he did his research and then rallied the people to build. The result was that the wall was built, to protect the people and thereby provide safe housing (6:15).

Nehemiah was cupbearer to the king. He used his influence in that trusted position to work for the good of his countrypeople. There was much opposition to the building project but Nehemiah stood firm and, ultimately, the oppressors were defeated. The people lived in safety.

Is God is speaking to you about injustice in some area? Aim to take time to 'sit with it'—mourn and pray—and then ask God how you can use your influence to bring about change.

Lord, there is much evil and injustice. Put on my heart and mind an area that you want me to concentrate on, where I can use my influence for good.

CHRISTINE PLATT

True source of justice

The Spirit of the Sovereign Lord is on me... to proclaim good news to the poor.... to proclaim freedom for the captives and release from darkness for the prisoners... 'For I, the Lord, love justice.'

Jesus applied this scripture to himself in the synagogue at Nazareth (Luke 4:16–21). This was God's third instalment of his plan for a just and caring world. First, Adam and Eve were given a delightful, luxuriant garden to live in, where they enjoyed God's undimmed friendship. When that situation fell apart, God chose Abraham and the Jewish nation to demonstrate his justice and character to the rest of the world, but they mostly failed to do so. Now, in Jesus, God reveals his master plan.

Jesus was the only one who could truly provide justice and 'proclaim freedom for the captives'. All of us are held captive by Satan, but Jesus 'disarmed the powers and authorities... triumphing over them by the cross' (Colossians 2:15). He has 'rescued us from the dominion of darkness and brought us into the kingdom of the Son he loves' (Colossians 1:13). This is the true freedom that Jesus came to inaugurate.

Now, instead of just one nation (Israel), people of every tribe, tongue and nation are invited to belong to God and enjoy his friendship. To accomplish this, God empowers us with his mighty Holy Spirit. We can be agents of his justice in this world, working so that others may also be freed from captivity and darkness.

Justice demands that everyone in the world be given the opportunity to hear and respond to God's good news. There are currently 6900 people groups who have no viable church. Eighty per cent of these are in the Muslim, Hindu and Buddhist blocs. Not all of us can go to these places, but all of us can pray and befriend those whom God brings to our sphere of influence. This is our role; God is not going to send angels to do it all.

Ask God to give you an opportunity to share your journey with Jesus with someone this week. Be an agent for God in his world.

CHRISTINE PLATT

Justice and mercy

'Teacher, this woman was caught in the act of adultery. In the Law Moses commanded us to stone such women. Now what do you say?' … [Jesus] said to them, 'Let any one of you who is without sin be the first to throw a stone at her.'

In this incident Jesus displays his determined pursuit of justice, yet it is interwoven with mercy. The woman caught in adultery was thrust before him. This was a blatant case of injustice. In Deuteronomy 22:23–24, stoning is the prescribed punishment only for a betrothed virgin, and both the man and woman must die, not just the woman. But Jesus doesn't argue the point of law; he gets to the heart of the matter.

With one sentence, 'Let any one of you who is without sin be the first to throw a stone at her', Jesus shames the woman's accusers. In their smug self-righteousness they were quick to condemn while conveniently ignoring their own shortcomings. With another two sentences, 'Neither do I condemn you. Go now and leave your life of sin', Jesus restores the woman and sets her on a better life path.

This was justice tempered with mercy. Jesus wasn't being soft on sin but was giving the women a chance to make better choices. I would love to know how she responded to that opportunity: she is someone else to have a conversation with in heaven!

It's tempting for us humans to point the finger at obvious sinful behaviour while keeping our own secret misdemeanours hidden tidily away. I've just heard on the radio about a man who repeatedly drives while drunk. He has already killed four people and is unrepentant. He is being released from prison today. I know what I feel like saying to him, but I wonder what Jesus would say. When we point the finger at someone else, let's remember that there are three fingers pointing back at ourselves.

When you are tempted to criticise or condemn others, examine your own heart and temper justice with mercy (see Psalm 139:22–24).

CHRISTINE PLATT

Passion for justice

I rescued the poor who cried for help... I put on righteousness as my clothing; justice was my robe and my turban... I was a father to the needy; I took up the case of the stranger.

In his prime, Job was a respected man because of his care for the poor and oppressed. No one's plight, however desperate, seems to have been beyond his reach: the poor, fatherless, dying, widows, blind, lame, needy, strangers and those being oppressed by the wicked all came under his protection. His whole persona demonstrated a passionate pursuit of justice for the vulnerable: 'justice was his robe and turban'. For him, alleviating suffering was not a part-time occupation or one to be done when everything else was dealt with. It was his passion.

William Wilberforce (1759–1833) is a more modern example of this driving passion for justice. For decades, his life and energy were consumed by the wretched state of slaves being captured in Africa and transported in unbelievably ghastly conditions in English ships, mainly to work in the sugar cane plantations of the Americas. Thirty-five to fifty thousand slaves were taken each year. This is how Wilberforce expressed his heart: 'So enormous, so dreadful, so irremediable did the trade's wickedness appear that my own mind was completely made up for abolition. Let the consequences be what they would: I from this time determined that I would never rest until I had effected its abolition.' Wilberforce also fought on behalf of chimney sweeps, single mothers, Sunday school pupils, orphans and troubled youth.

Despite much ill-health and harsh opposition, he persevered, with the help of many friends, and finally, on 26 March 1807, the Abolition of the Slave Trade Act was passed in the British Parliament. However, this only dealt with the trade in enslaved peoples; there were a further 26 years of struggle before the Abolition of Slavery Bill was passed on 26 July 1833, three days before Wilberforce died.

Lord God, put a passion in my heart for a 'cause, so enormous, so dreadful, so irremediable' that you want me to fight for. Help me to find likeminded co-workers.

CHRISTINE PLATT

Courage in a crisis

'For if you remain silent at this time, relief and deliverance for the Jews will arise from another place, but you and your father's family will perish. And who knows but that you have come to your royal position for such a time as this?'

Esther, a Jew, held a privileged position as queen to King Xerxes of Persia. This was at the time when the Jews were living in exile in Persia. Haman, an enemy of the Jewish people, hatched a plot to exterminate all Jews. Esther's uncle, Mordecai, urged her to intercede for her people before the king. This was a deadly dangerous mission as she had not revealed her Jewish ancestry to the king, nor was she allowed to enter the king's presence uninvited.

But a great injustice was about to be done. The elimination of the Jewish race would not only cause immense suffering but would also jeopardise the coming of the Redeemer-Messiah. God was not about to let that happen. Even though Esther didn't understand the bigger picture, she decided to risk all for justice's sake: 'If I perish, I perish!' (v. 16). She acted wisely. She didn't just blunder in; she devised a strategy that would appeal to the king—and she succeeded. The injustice was overturned.

A modern example of a courageous woman risking all to combat injustice is Rosa Parks (1913–2005), an African-American civil rights activist. One day in 1955, she refused to give up her seat in the coloured section of the bus to a white passenger after the white section was filled. Legally she was entitled to that seat.

These are her words: 'When that white driver... ordered us up and out of our seats, I felt a determination cover my body like a quilt on a winter night.' Three other black people all gave up their seats: Rosa was alone in resisting. She was arrested and charged, but eventually the city repealed its law requiring segregation on public buses. She became a catalyst for the civil rights movement to combat racial segregation, and they eventually won freedom.

Pray for God's strengthening for the persecuted church—for pastors and workers and missionaries who face extreme opposition, that they may stand firm.

CHRISTINE PLATT

The 'haves' and the 'have nots'

Whoever is kind to the poor lends to the Lord, and he will reward them for what they have done.

The writer of Proverbs explains that people fall into need for various reasons—some through their own folly (vv. 3, 27), through laziness (vv. 15, 24) or through having a hot temper (v. 19). His general advice here is that these people need to be left to bear the consequences of their own actions. That's more likely to bring about a change of heart than continually bailing them out of problems.

Others become poor through being robbed (v. 26). Some are brought to ruin by a foolish child (v. 13). Honouring parents are a key part of God's law (Exodus 20:12), which Jesus underlined (Matthew 15:4). Others become poor through having lies told about them: perhaps they lose their job or go to prison, unjustly accused (vv. 5, 9).

The gross injustice we face is between the 'haves' and the 'have nots'. Many who work long hours at monotonous jobs barely earn a living wage. It's hard to know how to combat this, but, at least, God's people should be proactive in petitioning our governments to use our taxes in the most productive way for all.

One result of being in need is that friends may desert us. As well as having an empty tummy, we have an empty heart and a downcast spirit: we feel as if no one cares about us: 'The poor are shunned by all their relatives… Though the poor pursue them with pleading, they are nowhere to be found' (v. 7).

What does 'being kind to the poor' look like? I recently watched a documentary about a UK charity that provides poor people with clothes, furniture, bedding and food in exchange for volunteer labour in their organisation. So these people's immediate needs are met, but they also experience the comradeship of being part of a team and helping others.

What would 'being kind to the poor' look like for you? How can you redress the balance of inequality in your community? Talk with God about this.

CHRISTINE PLATT

What's your life all about?

'If you do away with the yoke of oppression, with the pointing finger and malicious talk, and if you spend yourselves on behalf of the hungry and satisfy the needs of the oppressed, then your light will rise in the darkness… The Lord will guide you always.'

Everyone has been given a priceless gift—life! None of us knows how many years we've got. Some of us, like me, have probably got more years behind us than in front. The big D-day is ahead and we will have to give an account of our lives—whether or not we responded to Jesus' invitation to trust him for forgiveness and receive the even more price-less gift of eternal life with him; and the way we used our years and the gifts that we were given.

On what are you spending yourself? If someone examined your life, what would they discern to be your passions and your convictions about what is truly important? When an hour or day is gone, it cannot be regained. Many of us have times we're not proud of, but the crucial question now is: 'What about the future?' There is no point dwelling on past deficiencies; we need to focus on today and all our tomorrows. The hungry and the oppressed lie heavily on God's heart. How heavily do their concerns lie on your heart, or mine? God promises stunning returns to those who work for justice in his name and in his way—light on our path, his guidance, satisfaction, and fruitfulness until the end of our days.

C.T. Studd (1862–1931), a missionary to China, India and Africa, wrote this challenging poem (google 'Only one life' for the full version):

Only one life, the still small voice
Gently pleads for a better choice.
Bidding me selfish aims to leave
And to God's holy will to cleave
Only one life, 'twill soon be past,
Only what's done for Christ will last.

Prayerfully examine your priorities and activities in the light of the words 'only what's done for Christ will last'.

CHRISTINE PLATT

You don't have to do it all!

In those days when the number of disciples was increasing, the Hellenistic Jews among them complained against the Hebraic Jews because their widows were being overlooked in the daily distribution of food.

A situation of injustice arose early in the church's history, which had the potential to create division and bitterness as well as suffering for the Hellenistic (Greek-Jewish) widows. It would have damaged the witness of the church to those looking on. These widows had no family members able to support them, so the church had taken on the responsibility, but the food wasn't being distributed fairly.

The early apostles were responsible for everything in the church at this stage—spiritual leadership as well as caring for the needy. Fortunately they had the sense to see that they didn't have to do everything themselves. It was time to delegate, and the way they delegated is an example to us all. They didn't just dump the job on to the nearest willing shoulder. They gave clear instructions: choose seven men of good character and spiritual maturity. They gave the group the responsibility of choosing the men: they didn't impose their own will. Interestingly, all seven had Greek names, so it can be assumed they came from the Greek-speaking community and would therefore be able to represent their people fairly. The apostles commissioned them for the task. In so doing, they gave the seven men authority to make decisions.

When faced with human need and situations of injustice, it is tempting for some of us to leap in and try to solve every problem. The apostles knew that Jesus had given them spiritual oversight of his new church, and this would take up all their time. It is vitally important for all of us to know where to invest our gifts, time and energy.

The magnificent result of the apostles' wisdom is expressed in verse 7: 'So the word of God spread. The number of disciples in Jerusalem increased rapidly, and a large number of priests became obedient to the faith.'

If you feel pulled in too many directions so that you can't do any job well, then it's time to delegate. Talk with God and other Christian friends about this.

CHRISTINE PLATT

The equality principle

Our desire is not that others might be relieved while you are hard pressed, but that there might be equality. At the present time your plenty will supply what they need, so that in turn their plenty will supply what you need. The goal is equality.

As the church grew and flourished in Gentile cities, the apostles' teaching and example of caring for the poor became a hallmark of these new congregations. The Macedonian churches didn't only care for their own people but also 'pleaded for the privilege of sharing' with the Christians in Jerusalem (v. 4). Even though the Macedonian believers experienced suffering, their joy in knowing Jesus 'welled up in rich generosity' (v. 2). 'They gave themselves first of all to the Lord, and then by the will of God also to us [the apostles]' (v. 5).

This is the foundation stone of all Christian giving—first to God and then to others. We recognise how much grace and forgiveness we have received from God and, out of gratitude to him and desiring to honour him, we give to his people so that they may prosper and many others may come into his kingdom.

When God richly supplies our needs, that provision is not meant just for ourselves but also to meet the needs of those who don't have enough. At another time, when we are in need, others can supply those needs for us. God has given us an extraordinarily fruitful world to live in, with adequate food and resources for everyone. If we strove towards equality, then everyone's needs would be satisfied.

A horrific statistic is that 30,000 to 60,000 people die each day from hunger alone. Think about that when you throw food away. Also, 1.2 billion people lack access to clean water. Think about that when you turn on your tap.

Before we get totally overwhelmed, Paul gives us a helpful perspective: 'For if the willingness is there, the gift is acceptable according to what one has, not according to what one does not have' (v. 12).

Can you adjust your food and water consumption in some way? Even a small saving each week will enable you to give to those less fortunate than yourself.

CHRISTINE PLATT

Seeing as Jesus saw

Jesus went through all the towns and villages, teaching in their synagogues, proclaiming the good news of the kingdom and healing... When he saw the crowds, he had compassion on them, because they were harassed and helpless, like sheep without a shepherd.

It is fitting to conclude our two weeks of readings about justice by focusing again on our Saviour, Lord, friend and example—Jesus. We've already seen how he pursued justice in the case of the woman caught in adultery, and how that justice was tempered with mercy. We've also seen that he is the true and only source of justice. He defeated our enemy, so we now have an advocate in heaven who intercedes for us with the Father from a position of victory (Romans 8:34). We are safe!

We will be motivated to fight for justice in our world if we see people through his eyes. In today's reading we see that Jesus was travelling all around, teaching, preaching and healing. The task was enormous. There were crowds everywhere, with huge needs, but he didn't get compassion-fatigue. Compassion seeped out of his pores! He sympathised with their plight. They were 'harassed and helpless, like sheep without a shepherd'. Rather than being overwhelmed, he told his disciples, 'Pray for more workers!' The disciples may not have anticipated that they were themselves the answer to that prayer: he sent them out to preach, to heal, to raise the dead and to drive out demons.

There are many harassed, helpless and shepherdless sheep around us. It is perhaps hard for us to recognise their true state. Maybe your unbelieving friends and family members appear relatively happy. If so, the impetus for prayer and witness can lose its fire. We need to see people as Jesus does. He sees the reality beneath the layers of sophistication and the coping mechanisms with which people clothe themselves.

Justice demands that Jesus receives all the honour and praise due to him for paying the cost of our freedom. All of his flock needs to come home.

Jesus, take the blinkers off my eyes so that I see people as you do. I want to help your lost sheep find their way home.

CHRISTINE PLATT

Making links

Jennifer Rees Larcombe writes:

A friend of mine has the most phenomenal memory. She has a mind like a computer with a high-speed search engine. This is obviously a huge asset to her at work, but I'm also discovering that it has its drawbacks in ordinary life. We need to hold 'remembering and forgetting' in tension, because remembering can be destructive as well as useful.

Peter is the minister of a large Baptist church; he always stands by the door after every service to shake hands with everyone. He says, 'Two hundred people might say something positive about my sermon but I only ever remember the one person who says something critical. So I'm plunged into gloom for the rest of the day. If only I was better at editing my memory!'

Many times over, the Bible urges us to 'remember' events and people in the past, but we are told in other passages to deliberately forget things. So over the next couple of weeks let's explore what the Lord wants us to know about remembering and forgetting.

I went to Pippa's 70th birthday recently, and she showed me a card her daughter had sent her. 'It is more special to me than all my presents,' she said as tears of joy rolled down her cheeks. Pippa's daughter had listed 70 loving things she remembered her mother doing for her over the years—birthday cakes she had made, surprise picnics, beautifully knitted dolls' clothes and the endless cups of tea Pippa had carried upstairs while her daughter revised for her A levels. 'I'd forgotten most of those things,' Pippa said, 'but the fact that she remembers gives me the most enormous joy.'

Perhaps God feels like that too. Once I felt badly annoyed with him because he had failed to answer my prayers over something I was so sure must be his will. 'Stop whinging,' an unsympathetic member of my home group told me, 'and start remembering all the good things he *has* done for you! That'll soon cheer you up.' She was horribly right, of course, and once I'd stopped feeling cross with her I tried it. It worked brilliantly!

Lest we forget

Remember the days of old; consider the generations long past.

I've always known that I had a great-uncle Harold who was killed in World War I, but it wasn't until we approached the centenary of the Great War that I became curious enough to ask an elderly aunt for details. 'We never speak of him,' was her curt reply. 'He must have been shot for desertion,' I thought sadly.

I've always enjoyed those TV programmes in which people search dusty records to discover forgotten ancestors, so my brother and I began some research that finally took us to the battlefields of the Somme. Harold had definitely been the family's 'black sheep', but in his mid-20s he had found Christ and given his life to him. His passion for evangelism led him to train for the ministry but in 1916 he abandoned his studies and 'joined up'. Letters his comrades wrote later to his mother indicate that he continued to be an enthusiastic evangelist right to the end.

I would like to say that Harold became a hero by going over the top and charging through enemy lines, but he was digging a trench when a shell killed him. The trench was easily identified and, standing in it, we first felt sad that his life had been wasted when he might have had such a powerful ministry for God. Then my brother remembered Harold's newspaper obituary: 'As a preacher Private Sinclair showed considerable promise, but after just two months at the Front he made the supreme sacrifice.' As we thanked the Lord together for him, we realised that he, and men like him, had died to win our freedom to serve the Lord in our generation, even though he couldn't do so himself. Harold was faithfully doing what we are all called to do—to be like Jesus. 'Greater love has no one than this: to lay down one's life for one's friends' (John 15:13). I am looking forward to thanking Harold one day.

God doesn't measure a person by their success or achievements but by their faithfulness.

JENNIFER REES LARCOMBE

God, why don't you do something?

You walked off and left us, and never looked back. God, how could you do that? ... Refresh your memory of us... Why don't you do something? How long are you going to sit there with your hands folded in your lap? ... Don't forget us. Remember your promises.

I'm really sorry for the poor guy who wrote this psalm. He has just sur- vived a terrible trauma and seen everything he valued torn away. As he relives his frightful memories, he spits his rage, doubt and resentment into the face of God.

When I went through a similar trauma, I thought I couldn't possibly tell God how I really felt, so I walled up the pain inside myself until its poison began to seep out and spoil my relationship with him. This psalm writer had more sense. God always prefers us to tell him how we feel rather than burying our rage until it rots into toxic bitterness.

I learned that the hard way! For months I ignored God, feeling that prayer was a waste of time. As I've already mentioned, someone in my home group then told me to stop concentrating on what God hadn't done. 'Start remembering all the things he *has* done for you!' she said. That's exactly what this psalmist does. Suddenly, in the middle of all his angst, he firmly reminds himself of God's huge power (vv. 12–17): 'You own the day, you own the night; you put stars and sun in place.' Then he sinks back into his muddy pit of grief and question marks.

For ages it was like that for me, too. One day I'd feel fine and the next I was down again; perhaps recovering from grief and loss is like a very uncomfortable rollercoaster ride. In the end, I got a big piece of paper and wrote out promises like, 'I will never leave you' (Hebrews 13:5) and 'My God shall supply all my needs' (Philippians 4:19). Then I put it on the floor beside my bed so that his promises were the first thing I stood on each morning.

Lord, you do things so maddeningly slowly sometimes, but thank you that you never ever break your promises.

JENNIFER REES LARCOMBE

Why remember?

The women took the spices they had prepared and went to the tomb… Suddenly two men in clothes that gleamed like lightning stood beside them… 'Why do you look for the living among the dead? He is not here; he has risen! Remember how he told you, while he was still with you…' Then they remembered his words.

I wonder if my great-uncle Harold would be surprised to know I'm remembering him today by wearing a poppy. He probably never saw any in France himself—just mud. His memories would have been of trench rats, lice and the blood of wounded comrades. Yet I'm proud to wear this poppy to remind me of the millions of combatants who died in Harold's war and the even greater numbers who perished in the war that followed 21 years later.

Some people think it is time we stopped officially remembering the terrible tragedies of the last century, but perhaps forgetting could lead us into making the same mistakes all over again.

Remembering matters! By the first Easter morning, the family of Jesus and his disciples had been through three days of unspeakable grief and trauma and the loss of all their hopes and dreams. Yet Jesus had repeatedly told them he was going to be crucified and rise again three days later. How much misery they would have been spared if only they had remembered his words!

It is so easy to forget the things God says or does for us, such as special answers to prayer, verses that 'jump out at us' or pictures and dreams. People in Bible times often erected huge stones to remind themselves of particular things God had said or done. Rather than creating a 'Stonehenge' in our back gardens, keeping a journal works just as well.

Every time I feel that God has given me a promise, I write it out, date it and stick it to my kitchen wall.

JENNIFER REES LARCOMBE

Have you forgotten me, God?

She was in bitterness of soul, and prayed to the Lord and wept in anguish… 'O Lord of hosts, if You will… remember me, and not forget… but will give Your maidservant a male child, then I will give him to the Lord all the days of his life.' … And the Lord remembered her… Hannah conceived and bore a son, and called his name Samuel.

Recently I tracked down a friend of my mother who has lived in a retirement home for the last ten years. She greeted me severely with the words 'I thought the world had forgotten me!' She had outlived all her family and friends, and so had the other old ladies who surrounded her. One of our basic human fears is of becoming so totally unimportant that no one remembers we exist.

That wasn't Hannah's problem. She had a husband who adored her, but she was in anguish because she felt that God himself had forgotten her. It is so easy to feel like she did when we've prayed earnestly for years for something we desperately want and feel sure must be God's will. When nothing changes, we can easily be tempted to feel ignored and forgotten.

In one of those situations, I found two passages that made such a difference, I stuck them on my kitchen wall:

But Zion said, 'The Lord has… forgotten me.' 'Can a mother forget the baby at her breast and have no compassion on the child she has borne? Though she may forget, I will not forget you! See, I have engraved you on the palms of my hands' (Isaiah 49:13–16, NIV).

'Are not five sparrows sold for two pennies? Yet not one of them is forgotten by God. Indeed, the very hairs of your head are all numbered. Don't be afraid; you are worth more than many sparrows' (Luke 12:6–7, NIV).

Lord, it's tough to admit that you don't always answer our prayers as we'd like, but thank you that when you have to say 'no' you always offer us the mysterious gift of acceptance. Please give me the grace to receive it.

JENNIFER REES LARCOMBE

God's 'marvellous forgettery'

For his unfailing love toward those who fear him is as great as the height of the heavens above the earth. He has removed our sins as far from us as the east is from the west.

OK, so God never forgets us (even if we conveniently forget him when it suits us). Nothing can ever separate us from him or block us out of his memory—but there's one thing he does forget.

The doctors told my husband it was unlikely that I would last the night. Once he had popped home from the ICU to settle our six children, I remember the face of the hospital chaplain, George Swannel, hovering over me. At a time like that, you may not be able to talk but, provided you aren't drugged, inside your head your thoughts are as clear as ever. I was remembering past occasions when I had said or done things I bitterly regretted. I knew I had been forgiven but those memories still made me feel distressed. George must have sensed that because he smiled as he said, 'Thank God for his marvellous forgettery.'

I don't remember anything else until I woke next day, feeling considerably better, and found that George had written inside the cover of my Bible, 'For I will forgive their wickedness and will remember their sins no more' (Jeremiah 31:34, NIV).

'I thought God never forgot anything,' I said when, later that week, he reappeared by my bed. Again he smiled as he added this to my Bible cover: 'For all have sinned and fall short of the glory of God, and all are justified freely by his grace through the redemption that came by Christ Jesus' (Romans 3:23–24, NIV). 'Justified' means 'just-as-if-I'd never sinned', so when we confess our sins to him, he completely deletes them from his memory. He takes them away as far as the east is from the west—which means unreachable infinity. They are completely gone.

Thank you, Lord, for your glorious memory but also your marvellous forgettery.

JENNIFER REES LARCOMBE

Remembering—good and bad

Remember this and never forget how you aroused the anger of the Lord your God in the wilderness.

An angry God sounds alarming, but we need to remember that anger is often a reaction to very deep hurt. Yesterday we saw how wonderfully God forgets our past sins, but today we are reminded how much it hurts him when we forget them so completely that we sin all over again. Of course it is not right to keep wallowing in the memory of our sins but remembering objectively is a good way to avoid repeating them. In today's story, Moses urges the Israelites to remember how merciful God has been to them over their many lapses and deliberate disobedience, and I guess that, in order to appreciate fully his kindness to us, we also need to remember just how big is the debt of sin that he wrote off for us.

For Kirsty, remembering had become morbid. Before she became a Christian, she terminated her fourth pregnancy. At first she felt relief but then her actions began to haunt her. Even after her baptism, Kirsty still felt like a second-class Christian—someone whom God would never want to use or come close to. Shame began to spoil her enthusiasm for church and she stopped going. 'I'm not the right sort,' she told the friend who had first introduced her to Jesus. 'It's that abortion thing again.'

'But, Kirsty,' protested her friend, 'you and I knelt before the cross in church and told Jesus all about that—as well as everything else. He's forgiven you—but perhaps you haven't managed to forgive yourself yet?' Kirsty now leads her church's Sunday children's club.

Guilt is God's red-alert button, designed to tell us when we've sinned so that we can run to him for forgiveness. Shame often feels the same but it comes from the enemy, who just loves to accuse us (Revelation 12:10). Shame makes us run away from God because we feel unworthy of his love.

Help me, Lord, to recognise the difference between shame and guilt.

JENNIFER REES LARCOMBE

Negative remembering

And the people of Israel also began to complain. 'Oh, for some meat!' they exclaimed. 'We remember the fish we used to eat for free in Egypt. And we had all the cucumbers, melons, leeks, onions, and garlic we wanted. But now... all we ever see is this manna!'

The diet that consisted of three large biscuits each day sounded a cinch. Five days later, though, I was craving bread, butter and broccoli and had gained deep sympathy for those Israelite ex-slaves.

The manna was only intended to nourish them for a few weeks; it was their discontented grumbling that kept them in the desert for 40 years. Probably things would have been different if only they had kept reminding themselves how God had rescued them from brutal slavery and offered them freedom and future prosperity.

We sat round drinking coffee, all of us with grey heads and wrinkles—but once, when we were young, our children had been at the same school and we had made friends gossiping in the playground. We laughed about the oddities of the teachers and terrible behaviour of our sons, but the cheerful atmosphere changed when Beryl, looking bitterly at her zimmer frame, said, 'I used to love my tennis in those days. Life was such fun—back then.' We all began to realise how very different our lives had become. Most of us lived alone; our children had gone away and were busy with their own lives. Finally we all went home feeling rather low.

It was great recalling the 'good old days' but, when remembering is tinged with resentment and self-pity, it becomes toxic. I realised that Beryl had never been happy—not even back in those 'golden days'. She had always hankered for the past: 'When we lived in South Africa...' or 'When I was with my first husband...' So I made a cuppa, listed all the good things I could still enjoy in my life and soon began to feel much better.

The past has gone, the future may never happen, so seize 'the now': it is all we have.

JENNIFER REES LARCOMBE

Remembering by willpower

Why, my soul, are you downcast? Why so disturbed within me? Put your hope in God, for I will yet praise him, my Saviour and my God.

They say that talking to yourself is a sign of madness, but could it actually be the way to sanity? Today's psalmist was an exiled slave in Babylon, fondly remembering his homeland (v. 6), not with self-pity and resentment but with yearning nostalgia. I guess the upheaval of relocation and the loss of familiar places, family and friends had actually caused depression: he is certainly showing all the symptoms. He feels that God has forgotten him (v. 9); he can't stop crying (v. 3); he feels low and anxious (v. 5), drowning in sorrow (v. 7) and full of aches, pains and doubts (v. 10). Yet he keeps on telling his soul, 'Remember the Lord. Put your hope in his love and kindness.' In other words, 'You can't praise God now but I'm telling you to hold on because one day you will.'

I found this psalm a big help when I was depressed. I realised I was constantly talking to myself, saying, 'You're finished. God won't use you again. Just watch daytime TV and eat chocolate.' Instead I tried to tell my soul, 'OK, it's not surprising you're feeling spiritually dead, because you're like a daffodil bulb in winter. You're hibernating. But just wait— spring will come and you'll bloom again.' It sounds silly now, but it worked at the time.

There are occasions when we simply cannot think of anything in our present situation for which we could possibly thank God. That is when memory and faith become so important, remembering (by willpower) the things God has done and using faith to trust that he has our future safe in his hands.

Lord, please eject all the negative self-talk CDs that keep playing in my head, and help me to deliberately choose to play positive CDs instead.

JENNIFER REES LARCOMBE

Storing memories

'When my life was ebbing away, I remembered you, Lord, and my prayer rose to you, to your holy temple.'

My friend Bell received one of those dreaded late-night phone calls. Her only son, Peter, had been involved in a serious climbing accident in Switzerland; he was suspended, injured, at the end of a rope, while rescuers were struggling to reach him. 'The worst part for me,' Bell told me, 'was that I knew he had firmly turned his back on his childhood faith and told everyone he no longer believed in God. All I could do was pray desperately that he would turn back to the Lord before it was too late.' Five days later she was sitting beside Peter's hospital bed when he managed to say, 'I kept remembering all those Bible stories you used to tell me at bedtime, so I called out loud to the God you trusted.' Peter is now the vicar of a large Anglican church.

Isn't it painful when our children, or other young people we love, drift away from God as adults? Bell's experience gives me great hope for my own 'prodigal' and I constantly pray that the Lord will continually remind him of all I once taught him.

Jonah in today's story had very deliberately run away from God and had been caught in a terrible storm at sea, but, as he felt himself drowning, it wasn't his 'whole life' that flashed through his mind. All he remembered was God.

My grandmother, who had seven children, always told me how she 'constantly fed them titbits'. She meant that she was always telling them about the Lord she loved and knew intimately. 'I wanted their memories to be stuffed full of him,' she would add. She set quite an example to follow, but an unusually high proportion of her descendants are now following the Lord.

Father God, we bring you all the children over whom we have any kind of influence and we ask you to help us to 'stuff' their memories full of you and your love for them.

JENNIFER REES LARCOMBE

Remembering others

Through Jesus, therefore, let us continually offer to God a sacrifice of praise—the fruit of lips that openly profess his name. And do not forget to do good and to share with others, for with such sacrifices God is pleased.

Worship, for us, needn't just happen on Sunday morning. We can play worship music in our cars or kitchens, download worship podcasts and use apps on our mobile phones to prompt us to praise God every few minutes. Yet is that really all worship is? Today's passage reminds us that although God loves to hear us sing and speak worship, he is just as pleased when we worship by being kind to other people, showing hospitality (v. 2), visiting those who are 'shut in' in any sense, and remembering the abused as vividly as if we were suffering too (v. 3).

Jesus said that we would be more blessed by giving than receiving (Acts 20:35) but I always found it hard to believe that until one day when, as a badly overweight young mum, struggling to make ends meet, I realised I had nothing to wear for a family wedding. Then a parcel arrived. Inside was a brand new dress that I loved on sight and fitted perfectly. A note simply said, 'This will look better on you than on me.' I realised who had given it to me by the smile I saw on her face every time I wore it.

Sometimes it feels much easier to 'worship' by giving our tithe to church or responding to appeals for disaster victims, rather than by visiting a cross old woman or inviting boring Uncle So-and-so for Christmas Day. It helps to remember that all those things give God just as much pleasure as if we're singing in the worship group. Perhaps we are just being reminded that every single little activity of each day can be our offering of love to the Lord.

How about listing the leaders, speakers and friends who have most influenced your spiritual life, and writing down why you value them?

JENNIFER REES LARCOMBE

No! Not forgive and forget

'If you enter your place of worship and, about to make an offering, you suddenly remember a grudge a friend has against you... leave immediately, go to this friend and make things right. Then and only then, come back and work things out with God.'

'God's suddenly gone dead on me,' Susan told me. 'I love singing in the church choir but, recently, worshipping feels pointless.' I asked her when all this began. 'I was taking Communion one day and I started to have these terrible flashbacks. I don't remember my childhood but I always assumed I was happy; I'm sure my parents loved me but they live so far away, I don't see them now.' It took Susan a time before she could let herself admit that both parents had abused her.

God has a gentle way of helping us forget our bad childhood memories. He longs to heal the damage these events caused us, but he has to wait until the right time to allow the memories to surface. Healing comes through forgiveness but it isn't until we remember that we can forgive.

Susan found today's passage a great help. Communion had always been her most intimate way of worshipping. 'Perhaps that's why the flashbacks began then,' she said. 'Now I feel I can't take Communion at all because I'm so angry with my parents. There is no way I can forgive what they did to me. So I've resigned from choir because I can't sing any more while I'm still feeling so bad about them.'

After six months of counselling sessions, Susan finally found the courage to forgive her father's sexual abuse and her mother's beatings and cruel tongue. She even began visiting them regularly.

I'd like to say that Susan is back singing radiantly in the choir. Actually she was killed in a car accident, but I'm so glad she worked through all this pain and managed to let it go before she walked through heaven's gate.

Would you dare to ask God, 'Is there anyone in my past I need to forgive?'
JENNIFER REES LARCOMBE

Remembering: cure for insomnia?

On my bed I remember you; I think of you through the watches of the night. Because you are my help, I sing in the shadow of your wings. I cling to you; your right hand upholds me.

I sleep wonderfully now, but once a physical problem made sleep extremely difficult. In despair I told a friend, 'I'm praying hard about this, but nothing changes.' All she did was laugh! 'Stop asking the Lord to make you sleep,' she said, and jokingly added, 'Let the devil do it. Start thanking the Lord for all he has done for you—and the devil will let you go straight to sleep, because he hates worship.'

I guess David wrote this psalm during a sleepless night—not in his comfortable palace bed but huddled under a rock in the desert after escaping from ruthless, power-hungry Absalom. It had been a bitter day for the elderly king. He'd heard that his favourite son had raised an army to take Jerusalem and seize the throne (2 Samuel 15). Rather than risk terrible casualties by staying to fight, David and his household had escaped up the Mount of Olives and taken cover in the wilderness.

As he tried to sleep, he thought about the wonderful times of intimacy he'd enjoyed with the Lord in his house (v. 2). Had he lost that old life for ever? Then he firmly told himself that because God's love is better than even the most wonderful life, so he was going to go on praising God for as long as he had left to live (vv. 3–4). Hunger was probably keeping him awake, too, so he declared that God's love is more satisfying than any royal banquet (v. 5).

It was probably the worst night of David's very difficult life, but he got through it by clinging doggedly to the Lord's hand, knowing that he could trust God's strong right hand to hold him up during the following day (v. 8).

Lord, may I go on clinging to you by faith when my life is exploding around me.

JENNIFER REES LARCOMBE

A consecrated memory

I thank God... as night and day I constantly remember you in my prayers. Recalling your tears, I long to see you, so that I may be filled with joy. I am reminded of your sincere faith, which first lived in your grandmother Lois and in your mother Eunice and, I am persuaded, now lives in you also.

I love the way Paul talks about 'remembering' people in prayer. I often catch myself just firing names at God from my prayer list, but Paul obviously took the time to pull people into his memory so that he could pray and thank God for them (Philippians 1:3).

Trying to kick my habit, I've made a photo album of the people I want to 'remember in prayer' each day. Paul obviously didn't confine himself to a once-a-day prayer list, though. *Whenever* he remembered someone, he prayed for them. In today's reading, he is writing to his adopted son in Christ and sadly remembering how Timothy cried when they last said goodbye. Paul had loved watching Timothy's faith growing from boyhood, sustained by the prayers of his mother and grandmother.

If only we realised just how much our prayers can influence the lives of the people we love, I guess we'd all pray a lot more than we do. My grandmother started to pray for each grandchild as soon as she knew it was conceived. 'Putting treasure into the spiritual bank accounts' was what she called it, 'so that they'll go into the world rich in blessing.'

I remember promising to pray a friend through her pregnancy. It was a much-wanted first baby and she was 43. I was on holiday when I was woken at 2 o'clock one morning, thinking about her. 'She's not due for another month,' I thought, but prayed urgently anyway. Arriving home, I found she'd had a baby girl after a difficult labour. When I visited her she told me, 'At 2.00 that morning I was being rushed into theatre for an emergency Caesarean because the baby's heart arrested.'

Please take control of my memory and use it as a prompt to prayer.

JENNIFER REES LARCOMBE

Important forgetting

I gave up all that inferior stuff so I could know Christ personally...
I'm not saying that I have this all together... But I am well on my
way, reaching out for Christ, who has so wondrously reached out
for me... I've got my eye on the goal, where God is beckoning us
onward—to Jesus.

'Forgetting what is behind and straining towards what is ahead' (v. 13,
NIV). Paul tells us how happy he was to leave his days as a Pharisee
behind—the time when he tried to live a perfect life in order to please
God. Now he knows that it is his faith in Christ that gains God's favour.
'All the things I once thought were so important... I've dumped... so
that I could embrace Christ and be embraced by him' (vv. 8–9). I'm
not there yet, but I'm pressing on for everything he has for me. 'So let's
keep focused on that goal, those of us who want everything God has for
us' (v. 15).

The other day I heard someone say, 'I can't stand Christians who
dash from one spiritual hotspot to the next, always wanting a new experience.' Paul would willingly have gone anywhere if he thought it would
bring him more of Christ.

In Revelation 2:4 Jesus talks sadly about how we can lose our first
love. Obviously Paul was not in danger of that. After knowing Christ for
many years, he is still pressing for a deeper experience of him. I long for
a heart like that—a heart that is never willing to settle back comfortably
on past experience or gets bedded down in mediocrity, but one that
keeps yearning to know Jesus better and wants everything God has in
store.

Can you remember how it felt when you first discovered a deep, loving relationship with Jesus? Does he still mean the same to you or has
your enthusiasm for knowing him personally been dulled by the busyness and pressures of life?

---

*Lord, forgive me for so often being a stuck-in-a-rut Christian, doing all the
'right things' without any inner passion. Lord, keep me hungry for more
and more of you.*

JENNIFER REES LARCOMBE

Making links

Ali Herbert writes:

'Who do you say I am?' Jesus said to him. A question loaded with tension, with urgency, with intensity. The angels in heaven hold their breath. Peter the fisherman looks at Jesus and fires back, 'You are the Christ, the Messiah.' It's almost as if the tension immediately dissipates. The sunshine comes out again and the angels breathe a sigh of relief. But the Christ, the Messiah, hasn't finished yet: 'And you are the Rock on whom I will build my church.' Peter has confirmed Jesus' identity as the Saviour of the world, but we can't outgive the giver, and so, within the space of a breath, Peter's own identity is spoken and confirmed. He is given the name he will so desperately need in the weeks and years after Jesus' death and resurrection. He is given the authority to build and strengthen the baby church. His words and actions ring down the centuries to us.

It wasn't always like that for Peter. A rough fisherman from Bethsaida in Galilee, he seems to us to be hot-headed, sometimes confused, not particularly eloquent and apt to rush in without thinking. But more than anything else, Peter seems human to us. His failures speak to us as much as his triumphs. Are we more encouraged that he steps out of the boat or that he starts to sink as his faith begins to wobble? That he denies Jesus, out of fear for his own life? That he rushes in to cut off a soldier's ear in the garden of Gethsemane, or that, moments earlier, he was fast asleep even after Jesus had begged him to stay awake and keep him company?

We can recognise something of ourselves in Peter's frailty. We can also see Jesus' kindness and compassion towards him and know that we, too, can experience the same. We can know that, however uncertain we may be, the Lord of the universe has a purpose for our lives. The crux of the question we are asked remains as valid as we begin Advent this year as it was when Jesus asked Peter, 'Who do you say I am?'

Peter: the fisherman

As Jesus was walking beside the Sea of Galilee, he saw two brothers, Simon called Peter and his brother Andrew. They were casting a net into the lake, for they were fishermen. 'Come, follow me,' Jesus said, 'and I will send you out to fish for people.'

Picture the scene: It's an ordinary day as you go about the arduous business of catching fish for your living. It's hot, dusty and physically tiring and you are working with people you have known for your whole life. You don't have ambitions or hopes: things will undoubtedly carry on like this until you get too old to manage the nets, and old age doesn't bear thinking about too much. Then a man stops and looks deeply at you. There's something different about him, some intensity about him that is immediately unsettling—perhaps he's a rabbi of some sort? He won't want anything to do with you, a rough working man. But suddenly he's speaking directly to you, and there's a burning feeling in your heart…

So starts the story of Simon Peter. This day had begun in such a very ordinary way for him: he had had no inkling that by the end of it his life would be turned upside down. Yet Jesus is so low-key about the whole thing as he makes a gentle joke: 'Come and fish for people instead!' Simon Peter must have had no idea what Jesus meant, and yet there is clearly power in Jesus, something about his presence that utterly compels Peter to drop what he's doing immediately and become a Jesus-follower for the rest of his days.

God doesn't take extraordinary people and use them. He takes ordinary people and makes them extraordinary. Everything can change in the space of just one day. That call goes out to us all with the same message but in a unique way to each of us: 'Come, follow me—it'll be worth it.' How have you heard that call today?

Think back to the first time you knew in your heart you had to follow Jesus.

ALI HERBERT

Peter: the rock

Jesus replied, '… And I tell you that you are Peter, and on this rock
I will build my church, and the gates of Hades will not overcome it.'

Reginald Dwight becomes Elton John, Calvin Broadus becomes Snoop
Dogg, Cassius Clay becomes Mohammed Ali, and Marion Morrison
becomes John Wayne. Even these days we obviously find some meaning behind names—ones that are more glamorous or less silly, names to
be admired rather than mocked.

We find in the Bible that name changes are always significant. The
angel of the Lord calls Gideon 'Mighty warrior' when he is cowering in
a wine press, attempting to thresh wheat. Abraham is called 'Father of
many' when he cannot have children, and Jesus calls Simon by the new
name Peter (*Kepa* in Aramaic), which means 'Rock'.

For some time, these names must have felt mocking and particularly unkind as they were blatantly not true. Peter seems to be the most
impetuous of the disciples: he 'gets' Jesus sometimes but at other times
he gets it all horribly wrong. He is very far from being 'the Rock', let
alone from having a whole church built on him. Yet when God gives
us a name, it is because it is *going* to become true—however far away
it feels at the time. Peter must have desperately clung on to that name
through some very tough times.

We often give ourselves names that are less than helpful, or others
have called us names that have stuck like arrows: 'useless', 'not good
enough', 'difficult', 'too much', 'boring' and so on. It seems very hard
to shift these painful words, but God has called each of us names such
as 'valuable', 'precious', 'chosen' and the most wonderful of all, 'daughter'. Sometimes we need to ask God to erase the old names and rewrite
the new names on our hearts.

---

*Read Isaiah 43:3–13 to see what God thinks of us: precious, honoured,
daughters, called, witnesses, and so on.*

ALI HERBERT

Peter: the son-in-law

Now Simon's mother-in-law was suffering from a high fever, and
they asked Jesus to help her. So he bent over her and rebuked
the fever, and it left her. She got up at once and began to wait on
them.

There is nothing so faith-lifting as to see someone healed or set free
from pain. In my church a couple of years ago, a young student was
healed in a prayer meeting of a very serious heart condition—and the
healing completely confounded her doctors. That was a wonderful
thing in itself, but the effect it had on the student group was electrify-
ing. Their numbers grew; they found a new passion for meeting and
praying and a new desire to press into the things of God as well as to
pray for others to be set free and healed.

In our reading today, Simon Peter is anxious about his mother-in-
law and has enough faith already to know that it is worth asking Jesus
to do something about it. We are told she had a 'high fever' and yet,
as Jesus rebukes it, the fever immediately leaves. She is well enough
and has enough energy to get out of bed to wait on the people present.
She has been healed for a purpose—to minister to and bless others.
Furthermore, that evening the news has spread around the village, so
all the sick are brought to Jesus and healed by him—no advertising or
persuasion needed.

Being a follower of Jesus does not make us exempt from sickness,
and it seems that sometimes God heals quickly and sometimes he
doesn't. There don't seem to be any easy answers as to why that is, but
it shouldn't ever stop us keeping on asking for healing for ourselves and
(as Simon Peter did) for others. And if we are healed? Then our natural
response of gratitude is to get up, looking for every opportunity to serve
others and pray for others to experience the wonderful healing touch of
Jesus too.

---

*Call out to Jesus on behalf of someone you know who needs his healing
touch today.*

ALI HERBERT

Peter: the courageous

'Come,' [Jesus] said. Then Peter got down out of the boat, walked
on water and came towards Jesus. But when he saw the wind, he
was afraid and, beginning to sink, cried out, 'Lord, save me!'

This short passage seems almost to sum up the whole of the Christian
journey. Jesus calls us, we step out in faith, things begin to overwhelm
us and fill us with fear, we call out to Jesus—and he rescues us. This
seems to be the story of my life at least, in an ongoing cycle. I have
faith for something, then I'm filled with anxiety (which is far too often
the longest of these phases). As soon as I call out to Jesus, I experience his comfort and presence immediately. He may not remove the
difficulty straight away—and notice that Jesus took Peter's hand first,
before helping him back into the boat—but I know that Jesus is with
me in the middle of the storm, which is what makes all the difference.

If only I could keep my head lifted always, my eyes firmly fixed on
Jesus! How glorious it would be to keep walking and dancing on the
stormy waters of my life. Yet, every time, my experience is like Peter's. I
admire his courage in stepping out of the boat in the first place—none
of the other disciples did so—but I also love to see Jesus' response
when Peter 'fails', when his faith falters. Jesus asks him in straight
terms, 'Why did you doubt?' (v. 31) and yet he rescues him, brings
him to a place of safety and calms the storm. Even though Peter has
not fulfilled the *possibility*—the 'what could have been'—still Jesus is
glorified. Again and again Jesus takes even our failures and transforms
them. He rewrites our stories and redeems what we think has been lost.

---

*Lord, thank you for calling me to step out of the boat. Give me courage to
do it, and, when I fail, forgive me and rescue me.*

ALI HERBERT

Peter and the glimpse of glory

While he was speaking, a cloud appeared and covered them, and they were afraid as they entered the cloud. A voice came from the cloud, saying, 'This is my Son, whom I have chosen; listen to him.'

What a strange day this must have been for Peter, James and John as they travelled up the mountainside to pray with Jesus. Luke mentions that they had become 'very sleepy' (v. 32), which is not the last time we will hear this in conjunction with the disciples and the act of praying. But they soon woke up when they saw Jesus transformed in front of them, becoming as bright 'as a flash of lightning' (v. 29). Moses and Elijah appeared too and talked with Jesus about his forthcoming 'departure', the word for 'exodus'—or death.

Jesus is having his own 'mountain-top' experience, and its purpose is to prepare him for the pain, horror and sacrifice that is coming towards him. Moses is entwined in the memory of God's people with the glimpses of God on a mountain and, of course, with the idea of 'exodus'. With Moses, the people were led from death and slavery into freedom, and Jesus' own 'exodus' will bring just the same freedom for all people everywhere.

The three disciples are clearly overwhelmed and the ever-practical Peter's first, bewildered thought is to offer to build a shelter for the radiant beings. But the cloud appears and stops him in his tracks, and they experience the fear and awe that always seem to accompany a true glimpse of God's glory and presence. Just occasionally, we will catch a glimpse of the glory of the Lord and all our words will be stopped. We will be still in the presence of our all-powerful and radiant God. What a place to be in!

Lord, let me catch a glimpse of your glory today. Let me be quiet in your presence.

ALI HERBERT

Peter has his feet washed

[Jesus] came to Simon Peter, who said to him, 'Lord, are you going to wash my feet?' Jesus replied, 'You do not realise now what I am doing, but later you will understand.' 'No,' said Peter, 'you shall never wash my feet.' Jesus answered, 'Unless I wash you, you have no part with me.'

Jesus asks us to remember him not with a theological theory, but with a meal that we take together at the Communion table, in whatever tradition we choose—whether with a home-baked loaf, silver chalices centuries old, wafers, sliced bread or plastic beakers. It is a physical action that has echoed down to us from 2000 years ago, which we share with every other Jesus-follower.

With this meal comes another action—foot-washing. By doing this, Jesus is reiterating the point that he has already made so many times: the first will be last; the leader must be the servant; the characteristic of his follower is that of humility and preferring others. This idea is still so shocking to Peter that he at first refuses to have his feet washed. Surely it's not appropriate for a leader to do a job so lowly and humiliating?

The foot-washing is a sign that Jesus will deal intimately with each of us, that he will get down into the dirt and mess and muddle of our lives and bring cleansing and restoration and refreshment. Sometimes we feel too ashamed to allow Jesus to get near us. We'd prefer to keep some dark corners to ourselves, well aware of what will be seen if the light falls on them. But Jesus tells us that it is the only way. He will never be shocked or turn his face away from us, but instead will privately, gently and kindly cleanse us of everything that could keep us separate and apart from him. All we need to do is accept his offer.

Thank you, Lord Jesus, for coming down in humility and taking on the servant's role to minister to me in my brokenness. I accept your offer to wash me clean.

ALI HERBERT

Peter's desolation

The Lord turned and looked straight at Peter. Then Peter remembered the word the Lord had spoken to him: 'Before the cock crows today, you will disown me three times.' And he went outside and wept bitterly.

We can't doubt Peter's passion and enthusiasm for Jesus. He has left his livelihood to follow Jesus, stepped out of the boat, participated in praying and ministering, and seen Jesus do miracle after miracle. At this moment, however, it has all become too much. The fear, the turmoil of Jesus' arrest and the exhaustion in the middle of the night have all overwhelmed him and he denies he has ever known Jesus. Matthew 26:74 even says that he calls down curses. Just as Jesus is about to be mocked and spat upon by the soldiers for being a 'false' prophet, his prophetic words to Peter have come true.

The shame for Peter must have been unbearable. However, I don't honestly think that many of us will find it in us to blame Peter at this awful moment. Instead our hearts reach out to him in sympathy—horrified at the thought of being in a situation like this, feeling the desperation of self-preservation, and certainly fearful that our response would be exactly the same. It is the stark reality of Peter's weakness and the fact that Jesus knew everything that was happening that shows us our own shame, and the need for the cross. We simply cannot make it through on our own, however well we begin and with whatever great intentions.

The amazing grace of God is what is on offer: nothing we can do will make him love us more or make him love us less. We pray for strength in every situation, and we fall on grace when we realise that our strength is not enough.

Lord, we share the shame of Peter over the small ways we deny you every day. Thank you for your forgiveness and the truth of your endless grace towards us.

ALI HERBERT

Peter's glimmer of hope

Peter, however, got up and ran to the tomb. Bending over, he saw the strips of linen lying by themselves, and he went away, wondering to himself what had happened.

Some years ago, I had a miscarriage and felt shaken to my core. We already had one gorgeous little girl and I hadn't considered the prospect that this could happen to me. Shortly afterwards, I was informed that I had miscarried again. I felt bruised and hurt, wondering if I would ever have another child. A few weeks later, I felt unwell and returned to the hospital—to be told that a mistake had been made and in fact I was 13 weeks pregnant! My husband and I were gobsmacked, confused and overjoyed.

In our wonderful, mysterious passage today, Peter must have been at his lowest point. It must have seemed like the eye of the hurricane—devastation followed by an eerie calm, with nobody sure what to do next. The women had continued their small practical rituals, trying to bring some semblance of order into a situation way out of their control. Then there is this glimmer of hope. The women return with the news that the tomb is empty and that two radiant men have declared, 'He is risen!' Peter runs to the tomb, full of questions, desperate to see Jesus and to know if he is forgiven and accepted. What he finds are the strips of linen that had been wrapped around the body—a sign that Jesus has not just somehow 'recovered' from his crucifixion as a walking mummified victim, but that he has been entirely transformed.

Peter's questions are not all answered on this day, but he is clear that something extraordinary has happened and a new day has begun. It's not just at Easter that we must run towards the empty tomb and remember, and remember, and remember that for each and every one of us a new day has dawned.

Thank you, Lord, that the power Peter saw in action on that incredible day is the same power that lives within us today.

ALI HERBERT

Peter restored

When they had finished eating, Jesus said to Simon Peter, 'Simon son of John, do you love me more than these?' 'Yes, Lord,' he said, 'you know that I love you.' Jesus said, 'Feed my lambs.'

There's a wonderful YouTube clip of a small, wide-eyed boy with his face liberally smeared with chocolate, denying that he has ever been near the chocolate tin. He has almost convinced himself of his own innocence! Sometimes, when we know we've done something wrong, we really go out of our way to justify ourselves—even when we know it isn't true.

Peter is given his chance to confess and be forgiven. The disciples have left Jerusalem and returned to Galilee ('Tiberius' in some translations) and have gone back to what they know best. The miraculous sign of a large, unexpected haul of fish opens their eyes to recognise the man on the shore as Jesus. They eat together, the meal itself bringing the remembrance of the last supper they ate together, and then Jesus gives Peter his great, redeeming opportunity.

Peter boasted that he would never leave Jesus' side and then almost immediately broke his promise, but there is no hint of anger in Jesus, only grace. Will Peter humble himself to answer three times just as he has denied Jesus three times? Peter has been a courageous follower of Jesus but has clearly shown his weakness—boasting in his own strength. Jesus knows that Peter will need to be bold as the baby church begins, that the other believers will need every ounce of his persistence and energy, but he also needs to know that Peter will only boast in *God's* strength from now on.

We all make mistakes, some truly dreadful ones at times, but we need to know that Jesus will always restore us as we turn to him and admit our weakness to him. We must not count ourselves out when we get things wrong. Are we willing to step back into the game?

Jesus, I'm sorry for the times when I have let you down. Please forgive me and restore me again, and give me the strength to get up and carry on with you.

ALI HERBERT

Peter on fire

Peter replied, 'Repent and be baptised, every one of you, in the name of Jesus Christ for the forgiveness of your sins. And you will receive the gift of the Holy Spirit. The promise is for you and your children and for all who are far off—for all whom the Lord our God will call.'

The story of the Bible is the story of people being changed—of ordinary people doing extraordinary things. The disciples (probably about 120 of them) are in a house in Jerusalem, fearful for their lives, dismayed by Jesus' departure and confused about what they should be doing. All they've been told to do is to wait.

As they are worshipping together, this is the experience they have: first, something audible, the sound of a violent rushing wind that comes 'from heaven' and fills the whole house; second, something visible—flames of fire that rest on each person present—and third, something physical. They are 'filled' with the Holy Spirit and immediately begin speaking in tongues. The experience of Pentecost is so raucous and loud that the group are accused of having a wild, drunken party—and there's Peter in the middle of it all.

Is this even the same Peter we've known? Suddenly he is preaching the gospel, eloquent, fearless, powerful, direct, wise and knowledgeable. Suddenly he is the Rock that Jesus has prophesied. It seemed a pretty funny nickname until this moment, but now it makes sense at last. He is able to stand up and say, 'We are witnesses' to Jesus Christ, and his preaching is so powerful that 3,000 people are added to their number that day.

What is the purpose of this infilling of the Spirit and transformation? It is this: to let others know that God loves his *whole* world—not just a few but everyone who will turn back to him, who will run home like the prodigal child. 'Come home,' he says to each of us; 'I wait for you.'

The gift of the Spirit is for everyone. At the heart of the Christian message is this: God wants us back.

ALI HERBERT

Peter in Jesus' footsteps

Then Peter said, 'Silver or gold I do not have, but what I do have I give you. In the name of Jesus Christ of Nazareth, walk.' Taking him by the right hand, he helped him up, and instantly the man's feet and ankles became strong.

In the 13th century, Thomas Aquinas (the Roman Catholic scholar) was shown around the Vatican by Pope Innocent II. As the Pope gestured to the great wealth around them, he said, 'You see, the Church is no longer in that age in which she said, "Silver and gold have I none."'

'True, holy father,' replied Aquinas; 'neither can she any longer say to the lame, "Rise up and walk."'

There is nothing like a miraculous healing for stirring things up, and today we see it in action. Peter and John are now leading a mega-church of 3,000, albeit without any funds or other resources, and they have the courage to return to the Jerusalem temple to pray, the seat of the religious leaders who had plotted Jesus' death. An outcast beggar is healed and Peter takes the opportunity to preach his second public sermon. Maybe unexpectedly, he begins by accusing those present of killing Jesus! This is undoubtedly true, but definitely a bold move considering where they are. The message is getting through in an astonishing way as Peter and the others step out in faith, filled with the Spirit and doing the things that Jesus did.

Have we sometimes swapped the Holy Spirit for resources? Have we put organisation, administration and material anxiety in place of the streams of living water that are offered for free? We must make sure the power of Jesus is always available for those who are looking for him, who are meek, poor, broken, humble, lost, confused, hurting and desperate. We are the people who know where true healing can be found. We may or may not have much to offer our friends and companions in terms of material wealth or hospitality, but let's remember to offer infinitely more to them: 'But what I do have I give to you…'.

'Come, all you who are thirsty, come to the waters; and you who have no money, come, buy and eat! Come, buy wine and milk without money and without cost' (Isaiah 55:1).

ALI HERBERT

Peter the bold

'We are witnesses of these things, and so is the Holy Spirit, whom God has given to those who obey him.'

Some time ago in Africa, a woman watched her missionary friend take three new converts to a shallow river and dig a hole in the sand so that there would be just enough water to baptise them. As each person came up from the water, they began shouting in utter, excited joy. The woman asked her missionary friend why they seemed so excited. The missionary answered that she had not been able to communicate in the tribe's language clearly enough: while they understood that baptism was about 'dying with Christ' and being made new in him, they hadn't understood that it was symbolic. They had thought that the baptism would actually kill them. The woman chuckled a little until a thought stopped her in her tracks: 'If you thought baptism would kill you, would you be willing to get in the river?'

Peter and his fellow disciples now know that their calling from Jesus may get them killed, and yet they are without fear. They have witnessed something earth-shattering, and no fear of human beings or of death can stop them proclaiming the incredible news that God has made a way for us to be with him. In verse 41 we are told that they left the courts 'rejoicing' because they had been counted 'worthy' to suffer.

It is unlikely that many of us will be called to be martyred for our faith. However, as our country continues to move away from its Christian roots, there are likely to be more ways in which we are called to stand up against our society and proclaim the truth. The good news of grace is needed just as much, if not more, in our broken society today as it was then. What are we willing to risk of ourselves?

Jesus said that giving everything up would be more than worth it. Read Matthew 13:44–46, his parables about the hidden treasure and the pearl of great price.

ALI HERBERT

Peter the apostle

But you are a chosen people, a royal priesthood, a holy nation, God's special possession, that you may declare the praises of him who called you out of darkness into his wonderful light.

Do you remember PE lessons at school and the agony of 'choosing teams'? How thrilling it was to be picked early in the process and how painful and humiliating to be left until last? There is an innate human desire to belong. We look with envy on those in an 'inner circle'—something that seems to happen even in churches sometimes. But here is the good news for each of us: *you have been chosen*; you are royalty, and you are part of the priesthood. I love the T-shirt joke that says, 'Jesus loves you. But I'm his favourite!' Of course the truth is that we are all his favourites, his daughters.

Many years ago I had a friend who had been in a biker gang and had become a Christian. He and his friends used to rock up to church in all their denim and leather gear, but what struck me, amid the long hair, ripped jeans and swagger, was this guy's scruffy jacket, which had in large letters across the back: 'Property Of Jesus'. That is probably what we need to imagine putting on in the morning—an overcoat that declares to the world, 'I belong to Jesus'.

Peter is writing to the scattered baby church in his role as the Rock, an elder now, fulfilling the promise that Jesus saw in him all those years ago. He knows very clearly what it means to be chosen, but he doesn't want to keep that experience to himself. He knows that it's a truth for everyone, people down the centuries who may be 'strangers in the world' (1 Peter 1:1, NIV 1984) but who eternally belong to the Lord.

Even more wonderfully, you are God's own 'special possession' (v. 9). Have you considered yourself in those terms before?

ALI HERBERT

Peter remembers

We also have the prophetic message as something completely reliable, and you will do well to pay attention to it, as to a light shining in a dark place, until the day dawns and the morning star rises in your hearts.

When my husband Nick and I go away for a day or so, my parents are often kind enough to come and look after the children for us—which both they and the children adore. However, there are always things that need to be done—books to be returned, parties to attend, food to be cooked—so I write it all down in (probably indecipherable) detail. I want to be sure that everything goes smoothly and easily for everyone concerned, that nothing is missed and everyone knows the plan.

This letter to the early Christians is pervaded with a sense of Peter's departure. It may be that, as this letter was written, the cords of conspiracy were tightening around him, but what we see is his determination that the message will go out clear and true and the new followers of Jesus will know the way forward.

It often seems that the words of the Bible really are a 'light shining in a dark place': the hope of eternity and of Jesus' presence with us in this world are sometimes all there is to cling on to. Some of us will be going through incredibly painful times at the moment, through grief and loss and hurt of all kinds, and yet the knowledge that Jesus Christ not only stands with us in the pain but has experienced so much of it himself continues to bring comfort, relief and healing. The knowledge that one day the tears and crying and pain will be gone is also a powerful promise to hold to. Peter describes it beautifully in the verse quoted above, and we can join with him in that longing and praying to see the day dawn and the morning star rise.

Peter's story has been a rollercoaster tale but finishes so well. Take a moment to consider your own journey with Jesus so far, and imagine him walking alongside you.

ALI HERBERT

Making links

Alie Stibbe writes:

I've always found Advent a challenging season. We're supposed to be preparing our hearts, minds and spirits as we wait and prepare for the celebration of the birth of Christ. Like many other mothers, though, over the years I have tended to spend the last few weeks of the run-up to Christmas rushing around preparing for the secular side of what should be a holy feast, rather than focusing on the true significance of the season.

During the whole of the year before last, I learned the hard lesson of how to be still and wait while letting the Lord rush around behind the scenes sorting out practicalities and people in his own good time. We expect the same of our children in the run-up to Christmas, encouraging them to be quiet and patient and not to nag us while they wait in expectation for the special day that will surely come—a day of promised gifts, abundant food and fun.

Although I have always prided myself on living 'simply', during that Advent I was forced to *really* simplify. I learnt how sorrow and lean times have the strange effect of heightening our awareness of the spiritual magnitude of the promise of the Christ-child by focusing our senses on what really matters—the inner work of the Spirit in our souls as we wait for God.

Not wanting to lose my recaptured glimpse of expectant simplicity, I have determined to ensure that the lessons of that year are kept every Advent, so that I can be still and wait for God in the midst of the materialistic whirlwind that will inevitably accelerate in the world around me. I have been privileged to be invited to share two weeks of this journey with you. We are going to spend our time in the Old Testament, looking at what it means to wait expectantly for God and how an expectant attitude works to cultivate growth that is visible in both our inner and our outer lives. I have avoided moving into the New Testament because the notion of 'waiting' in that context is more to do with expecting the return of Christ in glory. I hope you will come away from these studies with the birth of a new facet of your life in Christ that will carry you into the new year and beyond.

Seek his face

I remain confident of this: I will see the goodness of the Lord in the land of the living. Wait for the Lord; be strong and take heart and wait for the Lord.

I've never been very good at waiting: I've always wanted things done 'yesterday'. I now know that this tendency in me was due to a desire to control my immediate environment—and the people around me—because I had a deep-seated sense of insecurity festering in my heart that had been growing for several decades. I thought that if everything was ordered, in control and sorted out, then nothing could hurt me. What a confession, and how wrong I was! Our security is supposed to be in Christ, and I had not realised how I had slowly lost my grip on that truth over the years.

Strangely enough, as that truth was reborn in my life, my worst unspoken fear came to pass: my husband left us unexpectedly. In the dark uncertainty of the days that followed, I gradually came to a place where I could say with the psalmist, 'The Lord is my light and my salvation—whom shall I fear? The Lord is the stronghold of my life—of whom shall I be afraid?' (v. 1). In such a situation, there was no point wanting everything sorted out 'yesterday': it wasn't possible. Even small practical amendments with utility providers can take three months to process.

In the midst of all the changes, I eventually found myself assured that I would get through it. I would 'see the goodness of the Lord in the land of the living'—I just had to wait. Many times I saw that something had been delayed so that something else had time to happen, which turned a situation to my benefit. If the Lord makes you wait, it is because he is working on things behind the scenes that you don't need to know about—so be strong, seek his face, and wait.

Lord, we are no good at waiting. In waiting for good things to come to us or bad things to pass, teach us to seek your face so that we can be strengthened for the duration.

ALIE STIBBE

Latent strength

But they that wait upon the Lord shall renew their strength; they shall mount up with wings as eagles; they shall run, and not be weary; and they shall walk, and not faint.

As I am a translator, I like to look at the origins of words: we can learn much from the original that is lost in translation. In the Old Testament, the English verb 'wait' can be the translation of four different Hebrew verbs. In the verse quoted above, it translates *qavah*, which has its origins in the twisting and stretching actions used to weave together the strands of a rope. It has the connation of strength and the tension felt during endurance.

It is common knowledge that twisted fibres make a strong strand of rope and that a three-stranded rope is very strong indeed (see Ecclesiastes 4:12), but what has rope got to do with today's reading? The clue lies in the awareness that waiting on the Lord results in our strength being renewed. A rope waiting to be used does not look strong; it is quite limp, but it has latent strength hidden inside it. If you anchor one end and put strain on the other, the strength of the rope is, metaphorically speaking, 'renewed' in that it springs into evidence once put under tension.

The poetic nature of this verse extends further in that 'mounting up', 'running' and 'walking' depict the three strands of the rope in action. When we look to the Lord and trust in him during times of difficulty, his power at work in us springs forth. We find we have inner resources to cope with our situation that we did not realise we had, and strength to endure under pressure. So this verse is not about resting and conserving strength so we can exert ourselves later, but about accessing the spiritual power and physical and mental stamina that are ours when we face each day with the Lord at our right hand.

Lord God, may my heart be so entwined with yours that when I am under pressure, your strength within me springs forth and holds me fast.

ALIE STIBBE

There is waiting… and waiting

Out of the depths I cry to you, Lord; Lord, hear my voice… I wait for the Lord, my whole being waits, and in his word I put my hope.

The verses that form today's reading are a cry of desperation from someone who has hit rock bottom. Perhaps the author was in a bad situation of his own making, due to some wrongdoing—maybe David after he had committed murder and adultery, and lost the child of that union. However, it could just as easily be the cry of anyone in any unbearable situation that life has thrown at them. This psalm meant a lot to me when I was struggling with post-natal depression, feeling as if I was sinking helplessly into the dark depths of the sea. Yet in his time of desperation the psalmist chooses to wait for the Lord, and to wait with his whole being (v. 5).

The Hebrew verb here is *qavah*, as in yesterday's reading, but here the sense is more about endurance through an extended period of soul-felt anguish. Perhaps the connotation of a twisted rope reflects the way the psalmist's guts feel in the situation.

The key to the whole psalm, however, comes at the end of verse 5, where the psalmist declares, 'In his word I put my hope.' This phrase contains the second most often-used Hebrew verb for 'wait', *yachal*, which means to 'hope', 'wait expectantly' or 'trust'. That is what the psalmist is doing—waiting expectantly for the Lord to keep his word, trusting him to be true to his character and pronounce his forgiveness so that the offender can be at peace and return to serving the Lord. Of course, in Christ we can experience God's forgiveness as soon as we ask, but our feelings sometimes take time to catch up: we also have to forgive ourselves. So while we wait/endure in the Lord's strength, we can also wait/trust that he will come through for us.

Lord, when we have to endure prolonged anguish of heart, soul and mind, help us wait hopefully and trustingly, knowing that you will have mercy on us according to your word.

ALIE STIBBE

As sure as the sunrise

I wait for the Lord more than watchmen wait for the morning, more than watchmen wait for the morning. Israel, put your hope in the Lord, for with the Lord is unfailing love and with him is full redemption.

Today's reading is quite short, being the final three verses of the psalm we looked at yesterday. I wanted to spend some time looking at these verses because the image of watchmen waiting for the morning is evocative. I don't know about you, but the nights I have spent wide awake with something nagging at my mind have been some of the longest nights in my life; I have longed for the morning and the hands of my alarm clock have seemed to stand still. At least I have been wrapped up in a warm duvet while I have wrestled with my thoughts, rather than pacing backwards and forwards on a cold rampart, stamping my feet to keep warm while I strain to see the first rays of light leaking across the horizon.

At these times, perhaps it is not the literal night that is long, but something else we are caught up in—perhaps purchasing a house, caught in a chain; undergoing treatment for a debilitating illness; a period of unemployment in which the right job never seems to surface; a complicated divorce in which the paperwork takes for ever. Whatever the situation, we want it to be over; we want to be relieved of the interminable waiting.

The wonderful thing about waiting for the Lord in these types of situation is that we know he will act, even if he seems to us to be taking his time about it. We can wait expectantly and in hope for what the Lord is going to do in our lives, because we know that, as sure as the sun rises each morning, we will see his redemption. His love for us never fails. Hold on in there and watch in wonder; the darkness will lighten in God's good time.

Lord, thank you for your unfailing love. Thank you that when what we are waiting for seems so far off, we can be sure that we will know your redemption.

ALIE STIBBE

Timely delays

But the eyes of the Lord are on those who fear him, on those whose hope [*yachal*] is in his unfailing love, to deliver them from death and keep them alive in famine. We wait in hope [*chakah*] for the Lord; he is our help and our shield.

Last year I rescued a six-month-old pug. My youngest son and I took our current pug on the Underground into London and collected our new addition on a street corner outside a grey tower block. Travelling home on the Tube would be an ordeal, so my daughter's boyfriend had offered to collect us after work.

We sat and waited. We had coffee and waited. His TV shoot over-ran, so we moved into the shade and waited. We sat on the pavement and waited. There was a further delay. We sat at the now-empty tables outside the bistro and waited. It was getting dark. Suddenly, just as we were about to give up hope and call a taxi, the white van appeared and we were whisked away to the safety of home.

How like our spiritual lives that experience can be! Sometimes we face situations where we are doing well at waiting in confident and expectant hope on the Lord because we trust in his promises—and then things take longer than expected. Much longer. We get tired and hungry, and long to be back in a familiar environment. How easy it then is to get impatient and angry and consider ways of solving the situation ourselves. But no—we have to wait according to the original plan or we will cause concern and confusion (see Psalm 106:13).

This is when our expectant waiting (*yachal*) needs the added knowledge of how to 'tarry' (*chakah*). Tarrying is hard to learn and may seem like a waste of time—but we must not lose hope or confuse God's plan by choosing what looks to us like a good quick get-out route. Don't fret. Learn to stop and smell the roses while God does the rushing around in the background.

'Yet the Lord longs to be gracious to you; therefore he will rise up to show you compassion. For the Lord is a God of justice. Blessed are all who wait for him!' (Isaiah 30:18).

ALIE STIBBE

Waiting in silence

Be still before the Lord and wait patiently for him; do not fret when people succeed in their ways, when they carry out their wicked schemes.

Yesterday we touched on the idea that waiting on the Lord involves an element of tarrying—learning to hang in there when the temptation is to take matters into our own hands and hasten the solution to a problem. In situations like that, it is good to learn to enjoy the moment, because there is not much else we can do.

Today's psalm develops that theme further by using the verb *damam*, which means not only 'to wait' but also 'to be still' or 'to be silent'. We do well to tarry silently. How easy it is to fret when things aren't going according to our schedule, and moan out loud about how long we are having to wait. Then we start grumbling about how other people have got it better than we have. No one wants to hear our petulant words, and fretting robs us of the valuable character-building lessons that the Lord wants to teach us while we wait. I have found that the best thing to do is to tell the Lord how you feel. I make a list in my journal if I have to (see Habakkuk 3:17–18), but I keep that list between me and him.

Putting our concerns into the Lord's hands and renewing our hope in him frees us up to live our day with our hearts and minds at rest, so that we can do the tasks that need our immediate attention positively and constructively. When I learnt this lesson, I was reminded of Moses' words to the people of Israel, caught between the approaching Egyptians and the Red Sea: 'Do not be afraid. Stand firm and you will see the deliverance the Lord will bring you today… The Lord will fight for you; you need only to be still' (Exodus 14:13–14).

Lord, in the midst of my turmoil may my soul wait in silence before you and find its rest in you alone—for my hope is in you (Psalm 62:5).

ALIE STIBBE

The God who answers

All my longings lie open before you, Lord: my sighing is not hidden from you... Lord, I wait for you; you will answer, Lord my God.

The wonderful thing about keeping a journal is that in the quiet hour before sleep, when we review the day with the Lord, with a mug of tea and a biro to hand, all our sighing and longings are literally laid open before him on the page. I have long realised that there is no point trying to keep what I think or feel secret from the Lord, so it all gets written down—even the worst of it. Writing out how we feel and what we think about a situation seems to remove some of the power that the associated emotions have over us. When we see the words in black and white on the page, the magnitude of our passion attains more sensible proportions, our hearts and minds are stilled, prayer finds simple focus, the Lord's voice is easier to hear, and the way ahead becomes clear.

Once I have laid my longings and sighing out on the page, I wait in the loaded silence for the Lord. In these times—or sometimes when I wake in the morning—I have heard the Lord whisper to me about many things. One of the biggest answers was his guidance in helping me make the decision to call the town I live in my home town, settle down for the long haul (Jeremiah 29:5), and resist the circling thoughts that offered the reproach that I had been stranded here in the wake of my desertion—for what? I remember saying almost 30 years ago, 'Who would want to live in Watford?' Well, I am living and working in Watford; God has had the last laugh, so to speak. Be careful what you deride in your heart or out loud; the Lord seems to use these things to teach us valuable life lessons!

Lord, you know my every heartfelt thought. Nothing is hidden from you. When I lay my confusion before you, declare your answers in the ensuing silence.

ALIE STIBBE

What are you waiting for?

I say to myself, 'The Lord is my inheritance; therefore, I will hope in him!' The Lord is good to those who depend on him, to those who search for him. So it is good to wait quietly for salvation from the Lord.

Have you ever wondered what you are waiting for? Over the years I have met many people who have been convinced the Lord has given them a specific promise—they are going to get married and have children, or their business is going to be successful, or they are going to emigrate—and they are still waiting for this thing to happen years down the line. I sometimes wonder if our specific longings are just that—our longings rather than God's intentions—because the human heart is 'deceitful above all things' (Jeremiah 17:9, NIV).

As I write, I am caught in a protracted time of waiting. I have no idea what the outcome of this waiting will be. I get up each morning, do what I need to do to get by, and then go to bed again. The temptation to sink into despair can sometimes be overwhelming, especially for someone who has always been so goal-orientated. Now I can do nothing but wait, knowing that nothing about the future is certain. The only certainties we have as we wait are the promises in God's word that pertain to his person and character.

When we read today's passage, we can be sure that when all is stripped away the Lord is still our inheritance: he is the one who has chosen us, and, if we have welcomed him into our hearts, we have chosen him. Essentially this tells us that the Lord is enough. He is sufficient and everything else is secondary. So when you do not know what you are waiting for, wait for the Lord: he is and has everything we need. We can be expectant about our future without knowing the details if we seek to stay close to him, and quietly trust that he has everything in hand.

Lord, I often crave to know the specifics and hasten ahead. Help me to still myself under your hand and wait expectantly for whatever it is you have planned for me.

ALIE STIBBE

Hold your horses

Moses answered them, 'Wait until I find out what the Lord commands concerning you.'

Today's passage acts as a good object lesson to us. The Israelites are commanded to celebrate the Passover at Sinai but some of them are ritually unclean. These people come to Moses and complain about the injustice of the situation. That is when Moses answers, 'Wait until I find out what the Lord commands concerning you.' The verb 'to wait' in this sentence is not one of the verbs we have met so far, but *amad*, which means 'to physically stand still'.

I like this verse because it is so practical. How easily we can get distracted by the spiritual aspects of waiting on God! This verse brings us right back down to earth: we can almost see Moses with his hand held out like a policeman, ordering them, 'Stop right where you are!' There have been moments this last year when the Lord has burst into my daily walk with a 'Stop right there' command. Sometimes it has been a verse from the Bible, sometimes a whisper in my subconscious, sometimes a blatant text from a caring friend; but every time the effect has been the same—to haul me up in my tracks and make me stop before I rush in where angels fear to tread. By waiting a day, a week, a month, the solution to our indignant complaint becomes clearer and the Lord's will in the situation can be done.

I have had this lesson rubbed in so many times, now, that when I think I am about to rush thoughtlessly ahead, I refer the matter to a trusted friend—not always the same friend, but always one of the people of God whose judgement I trust. Like the Israelites, we may have to wait a month, but at least we act in God's time rather than our own.

Lord, when I'm feeling indignant, stretch out your hand and restrain me until I'm confident I'm acting in your will and in your time. Make me humble enough to wait when you say so.

ALIE STIBBE

Caught in the headlights

So Joshua said to the Israelites: 'How long will you wait before you begin to take possession of the land that the Lord, the God of your ancestors, has given you?'

Too much of a good thing can be bad for you, and waiting can turn from being a spiritual discipline into an aspect of fear. In today's passage, the Israelites had reached the edge of the promised land and stopped; they were frightened to begin to take hold of what the Lord had promised them. Joshua challenged them and asked, 'How long will you wait?'

There are times when we are too eager to rush ahead and we need to be told to wait (*amad*, 'stand still'); then there are times when we should begin to move ahead but our fear causes us to wait needlessly (*raphah*, 'delay'). The reasons most people fail to take a course of action are fear of failure, fear of being rejected, fear that something might not live up to what we expected, or fear of making the wrong decision. I've become fearful of trying to make a serious career move because I've applied for so many vacant positions and had so many rejections that I've started to believe the lie that I'm not cut out for anything better, that what I have is as good as it gets.

Although we should always be thankful for what we have, there are times when we realise we are caught in the headlights of our situation. If we don't decide to make a move one way or another, like the rabbit sitting in the highway we are going to get squashed. It took courage for the spies to go into the promised land and survey what lay ahead, but it was a start. Is the Lord encouraging you to look ahead and see what he has waiting for you if you had the courage at least to take a look?

Lord, in my waiting, may I not become so mentally and spiritually inert and fearful that I am inattentive to your signal to get up and move forward.

ALIE STIBBE

Bottleneck moments

Then Naomi said, 'Wait, my daughter, until you find out what happens.'

This verse was sent to me by a good friend when I found myself in a time of great uncertainty. I had no idea what I was supposed to do in response to the situation because I had no past frame of reference on which to hang my understanding or decision-making. Subsequently I have found Ruth 1:18 a good verse to remember when part of my waiting on the Lord has involved depending on other people to make a decision, or for them to do something and get back to me about it, before I can move on with the next thing I have to do.

The verb 'to wait' in this verse, *yashab*, means 'to sit down' or 'to dwell/have one's abode'. I can imagine Ruth finding it very hard to sit still that day, because she was waiting to find out if Boaz could claim redemption rights from his relative and take her to be his wife.

I have been waiting for a friend to seek financial advice and come back to me on a specific matter so that I will know if my home is secure. 'Sitting still' in a situation like this is a challenge, but in such situations we have to learn the 'dwelling' aspect of the verb *yashab* and lean into the presence of Lord. We have to set up camp, metaphorically speaking, because the wait could be for a while and there is no point fretting in the meantime. Eventually, like Ruth, we will find out what happens. We will be in a better frame of mind to receive the news—whether it is what we hoped for or not—if we have been abiding in the Lord's love than if we have been caught up in a mesh of anxious thoughts.

In the day of my trouble, Lord, keep me safe in your dwelling place; hide me in the shelter of your sacred tent and set me high upon a rock (see Psalm 27:5).

ALIE STIBBE

Don't have a goldfish brain

*And he saved them from the hand of him that hated them...
They soon forgot his works; they waited not for his counsel: but
lusted exceedingly in the wilderness... And [God] gave them their
request: but sent leanness into their soul.*

When you are waiting on the Lord for a long time and events are unfolding slowly with delays at each stage, how easy it is to forget what the Lord has done in the weeks and months—and maybe years—that have gone by. How easy it is, too, to forget that the Lord knows the plans he has for us and has promised us a future and a hope (Jeremiah 29:11).

In the Western world we live in a culture of instant gratification and we want everything sorted immediately; waiting the equivalent of a metaphorical 40 years in the wilderness is just not our style. In our forgetfulness, we can allow our cravings to grow until they are out of proportion. This is so dangerous, as the potential to veer off the path and miss the fullness of all the Lord has planned for us by not tarrying (*chakah*) for his counsel is enormous.

In the Sinai wilderness, the Israelites forgot that God had rescued them when their backs were to the Red Sea. They had stood still and waited for his demonstration of power on that occasion, but now they were unwilling to wait any longer for the full realisation of his promises. They craved meat to eat, even though God had provided miraculous manna. You can almost sense God's exasperation as he drove the flock of quails in from the coast (Numbers 11:31). The meat made the Israelites ill. They were struck down with a wasting disease also described as a 'leanness of soul'.

If the Lord calls you to wait, do not hasten to drag the perceived endpoint to the place where you are; the result will almost certainly be leanness of soul or a degree of spiritual death. Tarry instead for the Lord's blessing.

---

*Lord, forgive me when I try to hurry the birth of what you have planned
for me. Give me the patience to wait until full term for your blessing.*
ALIE STIBBE

Obey while you wait

Yes, Lord, walking in the way of your laws, we wait for you; your name and renown are the desire of our hearts.

You might ask what we are supposed to do while we are waiting for the Lord to work out his purposes in a situation. The answer is simple: walk in the way of his laws. In other words, be obedient. Just keep on doing the right thing, one small step at a time, and one day at a time.

This morning I was at my early cleaning job. As I went round with a bin liner, clearing the rubbish, I found a large carrier bag of French beans behind the inner foyer door. I picked it up and carried it back to the cleaning cupboard, thinking the beans would be great to take home and freeze for the winter. Then I stopped. What was I doing? Someone had obviously brought them into the club for a friend, who had then forgotten them. If I was the friend, I would be coming back to get them. These were not my beans. Besides, I have a bed full of beans in my garden!

I carried the beans back to where I had found them and continued my rounds, horrified that I had almost stolen something that belonged to someone else. The trouble is, I'm always on the look-out for things people don't want that might be a blessing to me and my children. In my tiredness, the sinful side of my acquisitive streak had surfaced and capitulated and picked up the beans. Thank God he pulled me up short, because his name and renown are the desire of my heart and I would not want to compromise that over a bag of beans when I know he has already richly provided for me. Stay rested and concentrate—and make sure you stay within his ways by doing the right thing while you wait.

---

*Show me your ways, Lord, teach me your paths. Guide me in your truth and teach me, for you are God my Saviour, and my hope (*qavah*) is in you all day long (Psalm 25:4–5).*

ALIE STIBBE

Wait deliberately

In the morning, Lord, you hear my voice; in the morning I lay my requests before you and wait expectantly.

Ever since I worked in a shop, stacking shelves in the wee small hours, the morning has become a special time of day to me. I used to cycle home as the sun came up and the birds started to sing, the whole day fresh and unspoilt by the hustle and bustle of life, and I was full of expectation. I don't want to lose that feeling. I still set my alarm ridiculously early, at 5a.m., so I can enjoy that special time of day when I'm bothered by no one except my sleepy dogs and the dawn chorus.

Morning is a great time for talking with God; somehow heaven seems so much closer then, so close as to be almost tangible. I lay my day before the Lord, read his word—and wait. This is what the psalmist in today's reading does; he too knows that morning is a special time of day to wait on the Lord.

The verb in today's verse may read 'wait', but in fact it means 'to look out' (*tsaphah*) like a watchman from a tower, or like a prophet who looks out across time and sees the future as God reveals it to him. It is also the verb used of the noble wife who watches over the affairs of her household (Proverbs 31:27). When we meet with the Lord in the morning, we are not to wait vacantly and routinely but to survey our day—and the day of those for whom we are responsible—with eyes enlightened by his Holy Spirit, so that we can pray, be open to the Lord's leading and plan effectively. Intentional waiting prepares us for what the Lord has prepared for us so that everything we do ushers in his kingdom a little bit more.

Lord, as I wait for the celebration of the birth of Christ this Advent, I pray that in the stillness I will come to know you in a more intentional way.
ALIE STIBBE

Making links

Christina Rees writes:

The notes that follow cover the days leading up to Christmas, Christmas Day and the last week of the year, culminating with New Year's Eve. It is a time that moves from focusing on the coming of Christ, even thinking ahead to Christ's second coming, to welcoming the baby Jesus in the manger. In doing so, it embraces both the spiritual and the physical reality of God—God with us, as one of us, and God other and beyond us. We are challenged to bring together our understanding and knowledge of Jesus as both God and human. In celebrating the birth of a baby, a most common and human event, we acknowledge and celebrate our humanness. In recognising that baby as the Christ, we worship the divine in awe and wonder.

The season of Advent is characterised by waiting and expecting. It is a season of looking forward with anticipation, knowing how the story unfolds but reliving the excitement and drama of Mary and Joseph's journey to Bethlehem, the birth of Mary's baby and the exultation of the shepherds and the angels.

Towards the end of Advent, we move from our waiting and watching into the days of Christmas, a time of hope fulfilled, gratitude and celebration. Christmas is a time for being 'present'. In English, there are three meanings of the word 'present'. It can mean 'here', 'now' and 'gift'. When used as a verb, it also means 'to bring', 'to introduce' and 'to reveal'. In every sense of its meaning, Jesus is 'present' with us. He is here, he is now, and he is a gift to our world, revealing to us the face of God.

As Advent draws to an end and we enter the Christmas season, will we be 'present'? Will we be fully here, fully aware of the 'now' and open to receiving anew the gift of God living among us? Life is God's present to us, and it is up to us to receive it with open arms and hearts. Where God acts, we are invited to respond. My prayer for you this Advent and Christmas is that you will be able to receive and accept more of God's Holy Spirit, and so be drawn ever closer to Jesus, who lives among us as the risen Christ.

ACTS 17:22–31 (NIV)
Camel, bird or fish?

'For in him we live and move and have our being.'

The extra demands of this season, delightful as they may be, can deplete our inner resources and leave us feeling drained. The experience of running dry, of feeling as if we have nothing more to give, can, sadly, happen all too often at this time of year, when it is most inconvenient.

There is only one way of ensuring that we never run dry, and that is to draw continually from God's Holy Spirit. Some of us are like camels, who go for long periods without taking a drink. Some of us are more like birds, who take little sips of water throughout the day. But we are not meant to be like either camels or birds. We are meant to be like fish, who not only continually take water in and out of their gills—they live in it.

One of the realisations that has been most transformative in my life as a Christian has been to understand that I relate to God as a being who lives *in* God. I do not only take God in when I read the Bible or say a prayer, or even when I take Communion. I take God in with every breath I take. The Bible reading, praying and Communion are all outward signs and means of helping me to draw more consciously on the life I already have in God.

When I began to see myself in this way, I saw the world around me and other people in a new light. My response to God became more confident—after all, I was already in God and God in me—and I began to understand more of the type of relationship Jesus prayed about after the Last Supper: 'Father, just as you are in me and I am in you, may they also be in us...' (John 17:21).

Source and sustainer of all life, help us to remember that we live in you. Help us to allow your Spirit to flow continually in us and through us. Amen

CHRISTINA REES

This little light of mine

'You are the light of the world. A town built on a hill cannot be hidden. Neither do people light a lamp and put it under a bowl. Instead they put it on its stand, and it gives light to everyone in the house. In the same way, let your light shine before others, that they may see your good deeds and glorify your Father in heaven.'

One of the most potent images used in the New Testament for Jesus Christ is the 'light of the world'. The first chapter of John's Gospel, traditionally read at Christmas, begins with the image of Christ as the eternal Word, and then quickly introduces the theme of his also being 'life and light' (John 1:1–4).

Further on in John's Gospel, Jesus calls himself the light of the world (8:12), and promises that those who follow him will not walk in darkness, but will have the 'light of life'. The light of which Jesus speaks can be seen as being wisdom or truth, and in the Jewish tradition light was also the image of salvation. The contrasting darkness refers both to lack of wisdom, particularly the insight that Jesus was the promised Messiah, and also to the darkness of being trapped in sin.

Although we think of Jesus as being the light of the world, in Matthew's Gospel Jesus calls his followers the light of the world. Jesus does not mean to imply that those who believe in him become the means of salvation or that they are the source of wisdom, but rather that they have the same Spirit within them as he had within him. Jesus is also saying that those who follow him can become living flames, revealing the same truth, light and love that he revealed.

Loving God, help us to remember that we have your Spirit within us, and help us to live in such a way that others are drawn by our lights to the greater light and life of Christ. Amen

CHRISTINA REES

Share the load

'Come to me, all you who are weary and burdened, and I will give you rest. Take my yoke upon you, and learn from me; for I am gentle and humble in heart, and you will find rest for your souls. For my yoke is easy and my burden is light.'

Preparing for Christmas can be exciting and satisfying. Buying gifts for our loved ones, cooking special food, seeing friends and family and sending and receiving Christmas cards are all potential sources of delight. The reality is, however, that the last few days before Christmas can become a joyless assault course as we just try to get everything done.

So often, when things press heavily on us, we turn into stoics or sentimentalists, but we are to do neither. Instead, we are to go straight to Jesus and ask him to help us carry our load. Jesus has said that when we come to him, he will give us rest for our souls and replace our heavy burden with his light one. There are times when we cannot stand under the weight of the yoke that is bearing down on our shoulders, and we are told that we don't have to bear it alone. Jesus is here to help and is continually offering us refreshment in the midst of our journey.

When the burdens of our lives start to weigh on us and begin to rob us of our peace and joy, we are invited to come to Jesus. He may have had the whole world on his shoulders, but because of his close and trusting relationship with God he still could say, 'My yoke is easy and my burden is light.'

Dear Lord, please help us to turn to you when our burdens grow heavy, before the load becomes too much for us to bear. Please forgive us for not trusting that you are always here for us. Amen

CHRISTINA REES

To what are you giving birth?

The angel said to her, 'Do not be afraid, Mary, you have found favour with God. You will conceive and give birth to a son, and you are to call him Jesus.'

Gabriel told Mary that she would become pregnant and give birth to a son. The angel even told her what his name would be and some of what his future would hold. Today, the day before Christmas, we think of Mary as she waited to give birth, having travelled to Bethlehem with Joseph, far away from the security of their home and families.

There is in the Christmas story a sense of intense anticipation, the excitement that comes when waiting to hear how something will turn out. In Mary's case, she gave birth to a son, just as the angel had said she would, and she and Joseph duly named the baby Jesus. In spite of the prophecies surrounding Jesus' birth and infancy, Mary could not have foreseen what would become of her son, nor could she have understood the immensity of the mission that lay ahead of him. All she knew was that she had given birth to a precious child and that God had a special role for him.

Whether or not you are a mother, it is likely that there have been times in your life when you have felt pregnant—perhaps not with a baby but with an idea or plan or creation that grew inside you until it was ready to be born. Many people, including poets, composers and scientists, have described the feeling of being pregnant, with their creation growing inside them until it is bursting to be born. In one sense, the life of a Christian is to be repeatedly pregnant, accepting whatever new life the Holy Spirit is growing within us and being willing to nurture it and bring it safely to birth.

Lord of all beginnings, help us to discern and accept the new life you are growing in us. Help us to trust you with bringing it to birth and using it for your purposes. Amen

CHRISTINA REES

What child is this?

But the angel said to them, 'Do not be afraid. I bring you good news that will cause great joy for all the people. Today in the town of David a Saviour has been born to you; he is the Messiah, the Lord.'

The words of the carol 'What child is this?' that we sing to the beautiful tune of 'Greensleeves' tell the story of the life of the baby whose birth we celebrate today. William Chatterton Dix, who wrote the carol in about 1865, wove into his charming picture of the little child sleeping on Mary's lap, guarded by the shepherds and greeted by the angels, the significance of who Jesus was and what he had come to do.

In three verses of rich and lovely poetry, Dix establishes Jesus as the Christ, the longed-for Messiah and the King of kings who brought salvation to our world. He includes reference to Jesus as the Word, picking up the opening image from John's Gospel, and, in a few words, explains the saving work of Christ on the cross:

Nail, spear shall pierce him through,
The Cross be borne for me, for you;
Hail! Hail the Word made flesh,
The Babe, the Son of Mary!

Perhaps it is the familiar lilting melody and the tender depiction of the nativity scene 'where ox and ass are feeding' that makes this carol one of my favourites. It is also probably the moving sweep of the life of this little baby, who we trace from the first embrace with his mother to his painful death on the cross, that keeps the carol from being over-sentimental or saccharine. In the final verse, Dix returns to the scene in the stable and announces 'Joy! Joy! for Christ is born', allowing us to join our voices with those of the angels and rejoice on Christmas Day.

Lord Jesus, as we welcome you once again as a newborn baby, let us also acknowledge you as the Christ and worship you as our eternal God and Saviour. Amen

CHRISTINA REES

Joy to the world?

The Lord upholds all who fall and lifts up all who are bowed down.

The days surrounding Christmas are supposed to be some of the happiest of the year. After all, this is the season of good cheer, when everyone is at their most generous and open-hearted. Friends and families gather for special meals, and the endless round of Christmas parties is played to a soundtrack of jolly Christmas carols and festive songs.

That's the way it's supposed to be, but the sad reality is that the day after Christmas is one of the darkest and most difficult for many people, especially for women who live with a violent partner. In the United Kingdom, it is recognised that, after New Year's Eve, Christmas Day and Boxing Day are the two worst days of the year for abuse. Even more tragically, thousands of children are involved, their Christmases turned into times of terror and distress.

In addition to these heartbreaking situations, there are those who have just been bereaved, divorced, made redundant or diagnosed with serious illness. Tinsel, glitter and smiles only deepen their pain and sense of isolation. Today, let us remember those who are suffering, especially the people we know. Where possible, let us open our hearts and homes to them and show them they are not alone, but that they belong to the family of God.

If you are suffering today, know that God is with you and understands your situation, no matter how desperate or impossible things seem. That's why Jesus came, to walk the human path and understand what life feels like from our perspective, and then to close the gap between us and God. Reach out and seek sanctuary and assistance if you need to. Above all, trust and believe that you are a beloved child of God and part of the body of Christ.

Compassionate God, bring comfort and peace to those who grieve, and guide and guard those in danger. Help all who are suffering to know that you are with them. In the name of Jesus who lived as one of us. Amen
CHRISTINA REES

A peaceable kingdom?

The wolf will live with the lamb, the leopard will lie down with the goat, the calf and the lion and the yearling together; and a little child will lead them.

This beautiful vision appears in one of my favourite passages in the Bible. Over the centuries, many artists have painted the idyllic scene in Isaiah's prophecy about what life will be like for the people of Israel who remain faithful to the Lord. These paintings variously show contented livestock nestling up to benevolent-looking wild animals, with an innocent child stroking or feeding them—without a menacing tooth or claw in sight.

In this scene, natural enemies live together and, instead of mayhem, brutality and death, the reality is gentleness, peace and harmony. In particular, the image of a child playing with a deadly snake, something that would normally be a terrifying prospect, becomes an icon of the world as it can be when all are at peace with God, with one another and with the rest of creation.

What has happened to make this 'peaceable kingdom' possible? The clues come earlier in the chapter, where Isaiah lists the ideal characteristics of a future royal ruler, who will be full of wisdom and understanding, justice and righteousness, and who will usher in a reign of peace. Many see the realisation of such a person in Jesus, who from the time he was a young boy was acknowledged to have remarkable wisdom and understanding and a passion for justice and righteousness.

We quite rightly focus on the birth of Jesus as the coming of the Christ, the longed-for Saviour, but at this time of year I also like to remember Isaiah's vision of all creation living in harmony. When the news is filled with tragedy and violence, and when I find it a strain at times even to get along with my own (relatively tame!) family and friends, it reminds me that I can either help or hinder the spread of that peaceable kingdom.

Merciful Lord, please give us your wisdom and understanding, so that we may help to bring about your kingdom of peace and love. Amen

CHRISTINA REES

ECCLESIASTES 3:1–11 (NIV)

A time to pause

There is a time for everything, and a season for every activity under the heavens.

This week after Christmas is one of my favourite times of the year, in spite of the fact that it is usually cold and grey. I think of it as a 'hidden' week, a time when I can quietly regroup after the busyness and excitement of Christmas and pause before all my commitments and activities start up again in the new year.

Christians are called to be generous, caring and giving people, but I find that by the end of the year I need to take a few days to allow my spirit to be refreshed. I think of this week almost as if it is a retreat. I choose to stay away from the shops and the sales and, instead, spend time with my family and by myself. I often go out for long walks, breathing in the crispness of the air and burning off a few of the extra calories I have inevitably (and happily!) consumed.

This is the time when I give thanks for all that I have been given in life and for all that I am. This is when I allow my mind to freewheel, dancing through thoughts and memories as I become aware of them. It is a time to remember all the people I love, perhaps especially those who are no longer here. Above all, it is a chance to take 'time out', to be released from counting minutes and hours and meeting deadlines. I read books and magazines; I watch films; I sit and talk with my family; I potter and tidy a bit.

By the end of the week, my heart feels lighter and my head feels as if I have more space for fresh thoughts. My body feels rested and more vigorous. I feel at peace.

Dear God, thank you for today, for everything you have given me and for everything you have shown me. Please continue to reveal more of yourself to me in the days to come. Amen

CHRISTINA REES

The challenge of forgiving

Jesus said, 'Father, forgive them, for they do not know what they are doing.'

Our expectations of ourselves and other people are possibly at their highest around Christmas: 'This year, I will finally have lost that weight… This year, I will be ready ahead of time… This year, everyone will get on…' Yet when 'this year' comes, once again we find that we still have a few pounds to lose, we have run out of time, and as for everyone getting on…!

Disappointment in ourselves or the behaviour of those around us can rob us of our peace and joy and leave a bitter taste in our mouths when we look back on what should have been a time of harmony and celebration.

Some of the last words Jesus spoke before he died were a prayer, asking God to forgive the very people who had nailed him to the cross. If we want to know what Jesus thought about the importance of forgiveness, we do not have to look anywhere else than at these remarkable words, made supremely significant by their horrifying context.

If Jesus can forgive those who put him to death, then we must face forgiving those who have hurt us. It has been said that no offence is unforgivable, unless we make it so. Being able to forgive, however, is not always possible. It is not even possible sometimes to forgive ourselves. Thankfully, we worship a God who, in Christ, has already forgiven all the sin and hurt and falling short that has been committed in the past, that is happening now, and that will be done in the future.

When we feel unable to forgive, we can at least pray to be willing to allow God's love and forgiveness to melt our hearts, so that one day we will know the freedom that comes from giving and accepting forgiveness.

Forgiving God, please help me to be willing to forgive myself and others. Where I cannot forgive, please help me to accept that you have already forgiven. Amen

CHRISTINA REES

Pressing on, letting go

Therefore, since we are surrounded by such a great cloud of witnesses, let us throw off everything that hinders and the sin that so easily entangles. And let us run with perseverance the race marked out for us, fixing our eyes on Jesus, the pioneer and perfecter of faith.

The day after tomorrow is the start of the new year. If you are like me, you will be thinking about making changes and setting goals in the year to come. Some of those goals will be connected to a future event, such as a wedding in the family or a new job. Other goals will be about the perennial challenge of considering how best to live as a disciple of Jesus Christ.

What is it that we need most at the beginning of a new year to help us achieve the goal of 'running the race that is set before us'? The sporting analogy in this passage resonates more vividly with us, after the 2012 Olympic and Paralympic Games, and the Commonwealth Games earlier this year. Each of us will probably have memories of our favourite athletes and events. The picture here is of a marathon rather than a sprint, conjuring up images of the endurance and perseverance of a long-distance runner.

In chapter 11, the writer of Hebrews lists a catalogue of heroes of faith but ends with the acknowledgement that, although these people did well, they could not attain the perfection that Jesus accomplished in his life and death, a perfection that transforms our own 'race'.

We must run our own race, each of us responsible for getting rid of as much 'weight' as possible, whether that is the weight of sin or of futile worldly distractions. At the same time we are called to trust that Jesus, by his death and resurrection, has already won the race for us. We are called to a life of both resolute determination and perseverance, along with complete reliance and trust.

Lord Jesus, please help me to stay strong and faithful, always drawing my strength from you and abiding in your love. Amen

CHRISTINA REES

A new way of seeing

Therefore, if anyone is in Christ, the new creation has come: the old has gone, the new is here!

Tomorrow is the start of a new year. Although none of us knows what it will bring, we can enter it with the confidence that, in God, our futures are held securely in love. We can also enter it seeing our lives in a whole new light.

After his dramatic encounter with Christ on the road to Damascus, Paul banked everything on what he had 'seen' during the three days he was blinded. He regained his physical sight with an entirely new spiritual vision of what life and truth was all about. Above all, he had a new vision of Jesus.

The man who had persecuted Christians with such hatred became the man who would spread the message of God's transforming love in Christ. Part of Paul's new vision was of the world reconciled to God, made possible by Jesus' death and resurrection. Paul also saw his purpose and the purpose of all who believe in Jesus as to be active agents in bringing about that reconciliation.

It is not just that we have to try hard to be good people and live as best we can, but rather that if we have opened ourselves to the Holy Spirit, we become part of the divine action of bringing all things back into union with God. We accomplish this by living 'in Christ', continually drawing in Jesus' ever-living presence, made possible by prayer and by breaking bread with the community of those who believe.

By seeing ourselves as a new creation, we are actually helping to bring a new world into being, a world in which all things are one in God. This new world already exists. It's what Jesus was getting at when he talked about the kingdom of heaven being *within* us, meaning 'here', and *at hand*, meaning 'now'. What we have to do is to become aware of it—and spread the good news.

God of new beginnings, please help me to see myself, others and the world with the eyes of Christ. Amen

CHRISTINA REES

Other Christina Press titles

In His Time Eileen Gordon-Smith (£5.99)
Five missionaries and seven children are killed in a bus crash. Where is God when
it hurts? 'I am different now—I no longer fear death.'

Who'd Plant a Church? Diana Archer (£5.99)
Planting an Anglican church from scratch, with a team of four—two adults and
two children—is an unusual adventure even in these days. Diana Archer gives a
distinctive perspective on parish life.

Pathway Through Grief edited by Jean Watson (£6.99)
Ten Christians, each bereaved, share their experience of loss. Frank and sensitive
accounts offering comfort and reassurance to those recently bereaved and new
insights to those involved in counselling.

God's Catalyst Rosemary Green (£8.99)
Insight, inspiration and advice for both counsellors and concerned Christians who
long to be channels of God's Spirit to help those in need. A unique tool for the
non-specialist counsellor.

Angels Keep Watch Carol Hathorne (£5.99)
After 40 years, Carol Hathorne obeyed God's call to Kenya. She came face to face
with dangers, hardships and poverty, but experienced the joy of learning that
Christianity is still growing in God's world.

Not a Super-Saint Liz Hansford (£6.99)
Describes the outlandish situations that arise in the Manse, where life is both
fraught and tremendous fun. A book for the ordinary Christian who feels they must
be the only one who hasn't quite got it together.

The Addiction of a Busy Life Edward England (£5.99)
Twelve lessons from a devastating heart attack. Edward, a giant of Christian
publishing in the UK, and founder of Christina Press, shares what the Lord taught
him when his life nearly came to an abrupt end.

Life Path Luci Shaw (£5.99)
Keeping a journal can enrich life as we live it, and bring it all back later. Luci Shaw
shows how a journal can also help us grow in our walk with God.

Other BRF titles

Creative Prayer Ideas Claire Daniel (£8.99)
Prayer is a vital part of the Christian life but people often struggle with actually getting on and doing it. This book offers 80 imaginative and creative ideas for setting up 'prayer stations', practical ways of praying that involve the senses—touching, tasting, smelling, seeing and hearing, rather than simply reflecting—as we bring our hopes, fears, dreams and doubts to God. Developed from material tried and tested with small groups, the ideas provide activities ranging from bubble prayers to clay pot prayers (via just about everything else in between), and have been designed to be used with grown-ups of all ages.

Journalling the Bible Corin Child (£7.99)
The spiritual discipline of journalling has become increasingly popular in recent years and this book shows how it can fruitfully overlap with creative writing to provide an original way of engaging with the Bible. 'Bible study' is usually taken to mean 'reading and discussing'—but writing offers a different way of interacting with the text, generating new insights and application even from the most familiar of passages. *Journalling the Bible* offers 40 writing/journalling exercises that have been tested in workshops around the country, providing an imaginative resource for individual and group work and a refreshingly different way to become better acquainted with scripture.

Mary Andrew Jones (£8.99)
Mary is arguably the first disciple—somebody who lived in the world but also lived very close to the heart of God. In this book, Andrew Jones explores the different ways she is presented in the Gospels and also in Christian spirituality down through history, showing how her significance extends far beyond the Christmas story, to the foot of the cross and beyond. By setting her in her full biblical context, drawing on both Old and New Testaments, he also considers how Mary can be an invaluable focus for ecumenical unity, rather than a means of division.

Longing, Waiting, Believing Rodney Holder (£7.99)
This book of daily Bible readings and reflective comment covers the weeks from 1 December through to Epiphany on 6 January. As well as considering the well-known events of the nativity story, it looks back to those who prepared the way—the patriarchs and prophets of the Old Testament and John the Baptist and Mary the mother of Jesus in the New Testament. The book also explores the traditional Advent focus on the 'four last things', death, judgment, heaven and hell.

YOU CAN ORDER THE TITLES ON THESE TWO PAGES FROM CHRISTINA PRESS OR BRF, USING THE ORDER FORMS ON PAGES 140 AND 141.

Christina Press Publications Order Form

All of these publications are available from Christian bookshops everywhere or, in case of difficulty, direct from the publisher. Please make your selection below, complete the payment details and send your order with payment as appropriate to:

Christina Press Ltd, 17 Church Road, Tunbridge Wells, Kent TN1 1LG

		Qty	Price	Total
8700	God's Catalyst	____	£8.99	____
8701	Women Celebrating Faith	____	£5.99	____
8702	Precious to God	____	£5.99	____
8703	Angels Keep Watch	____	£5.99	____
8704	Life Path	____	£5.99	____
8705	Pathway Through Grief	____	£6.99	____
8706	Who'd Plant a Church?	____	£5.99	____
8707	Dear God, It's Me and It's Urgent	____	£6.99	____
8708	Not a Super-Saint	____	£6.99	____
8709	The Addiction of a Busy Life	____	£5.99	____
8710	In His Time	____	£5.99	____

POSTAGE AND PACKING CHARGES				
	UK	Europe	Surface	Air Mail
£7.00 & under	£1.25	£3.00	£3.50	£5.50
£7.01–£29.99	£2.25	£5.50	£6.50	£10.00
£30.00 & over	free	prices on request		

Total cost of books £ ____
Postage and Packing £ ____
TOTAL £ ____

All prices are correct at time of going to press, are subject to the prevailing rate of VAT and may be subject to change without prior warning.

Name _____

Address _____

_____

_____ Postcode _____

Telephone number _____

Total enclosed £ _____ (cheques should be made payable to 'Christina Press Ltd')

❏ Please do not send me further information about Christina Press publications

BRF Publications Order Form

All of these publications are available from Christian bookshops everywhere, or in case of difficulty direct from the publisher. Please make your selection below, complete the payment details and send your order with payment as appropriate to:

BRF, 15 The Chambers, Vineyard, Abingdon OX14 3FE

		Qty	Price	Total
688 7	Creative Prayer Ideas	____	£8.99	____
736 5	Journalling the Bible	____	£7.99	____
651 1	Mary	____	£8.99	____
756 3	Longing, Waiting, Believing	____	£7.99	____

POSTAGE AND PACKING CHARGES				
	UK	Europe	Surface	Air Mail
£7.00 & under	£1.25	£3.00	£3.50	£5.50
£7.01–£29.99	£2.25	£5.50	£6.50	£10.00
£30.00 & over	free	prices on request		

Total cost of books   £ ____
Postage and Packing   £ ____
TOTAL   £ ____

All prices are correct at time of going to press, are subject to the prevailing rate of VAT and may be subject to change without prior warning.

Name _____

Address _____

_____ Postcode _____

Phone _____ Email _____

Total enclosed £ _____ (cheques should be made payable to 'BRF')

Please charge my Visa ❏   Mastercard ❏   with £ _____

Card no. ⬚⬚⬚⬚⬚⬚⬚⬚⬚⬚⬚⬚⬚⬚⬚⬚

Expires ⬚⬚⬚   Security code ⬚⬚⬚

Signature _____
(essential if paying by card)

❏ Please do not send me further information about BRF publications

Visit the BRF website at www.brf.org.uk

BRF is a Registered Charity

Subscription Information

Each issue of *Day by Day with God* is available from Christian bookshops everywhere. Copies may also be available through your church Book Agent or from the person who distributes Bible reading notes in your church.

Alternatively you may obtain *Day by Day with God* on subscription direct from the publishers. There are two kinds of subscription:

Individual Subscriptions are for four copies or less, and include postage and packing. To order an annual Individual Subscription, please complete the details on page 144 and send the coupon with payment to BRF in Abingdon. You can also use the form to order a Gift Subscription for a friend.

Church Subscriptions are for five copies or more, sent to one address, and are supplied post free. Church Subscriptions run from 1 May to 30 April each year and are invoiced annually. To order a Church Subscription, please complete the details opposite and send the coupon to BRF in Abingdon. You will receive an invoice with the first issue of notes.

All subscription enquiries should be directed to:

BRF
15 The Chambers
Vineyard
Abingdon
OX14 3FE

Tel: 01865 319700
Fax: 01865 319701
E-mail: subscriptions@brf.org.uk